2ND EDITION

BUILDING BLOCKS *for* RELATIONSHIPS

Qualities for Christian Living

GASPAR GARCIA

BLUEPRINT PRESS INTERNATIONALE

ISBN
978-1-961117-27-3 (Paperback)
978-1-961117-28-0 (eBook)
978-1-961117-26-6 (Hardcover)

DEDICATION

This Book is about establishing relationships according to Bible precepts. Many years ago, my concept of relationship did not extend beyond what I could get for myself in my transactions with others. If you are hearing this for the first time, you might think that I was normal. I may have been normal but I was far from realizing the Father's will for relationships in my life. My sense of relationship was very skewed and self-centered. Then I met a woman I wanted to spend my life with. Her sense of relationship, marriage, family and commitment were foreign to me, yet intriguing. As we both grew in the Lord, her ways became more apparent and clearer to me as I came to understand her purpose in light of the living Word. Her connection to me changed my perspective on relationships and gave me a new life as we continued together to learn more each day of God's ways day-by-day.

Today, she is my wife and has been the completer and life partner who continues to teach me more about relating to her and relating to others through Christ. I dedicate this Book to my wife, Terry, who has been a source of total support and my cheerleader in everything and anything I choose to do, especially in writing this book.

ACKNOWLEDGEMENTS

I want to thank the people who have made this book possible. There are too many to mention, but each one encouraged me in some way to write this book. The most prominent are the teachers of God's Word who have over the years consistently guided me to new and greater understanding. Without their teachings, this book would not have been possible.

Specifically, I want to thank Reverend Vincent Finnegan who for over the past three decades has been a spiritual leader to me, my family and my many friends throughout New York state, Florida, and elsewhere. His teachings have been an inspiration that have led me to study the Word more intently. Reverend John McCave is my other inspiration and a good friend. Through his works and teachings, I have been inspired to search the Bible for deeper understanding and to be assured that biblical principles I have taught accurately line up with the Word. Another good friend and pastor to whom I owe much gratitude is Reverend Glenn Post who was my shepherd, mentor and friend for many years and the man of God who presided over my ordination. To these men, I am eternally grateful and look forward to an eternity of fellowship to come.

My single biggest inspiration for this book and the person who has given me the most encouragement is my daughter, Jillann Gonzalez, who has been my technical advisor, editor and moral supporter. While proof reading, she would often pause and apply or question herself about the precepts in her own life. Her feedback was substantial and a great help. I want to thank Jill for her critical contributions and especially for reading the manuscript many times over, the last time for grammar and conformity. A book such as this is written to give instruction on how to apply concepts that are new to us, and it requires many bullet points, indentations, and text boxes that present a number of opportunities for inconsistency. To a large degree, Jill has taken over that dreaded responsibility and has done a remarkable job with it. I am ever so thankful for Jill and all her assistance.

This work is in great part a result of seminars conducted for members of our church, Church of Divine Grace, and other friends. The teachings on relationships originated from marriage and family counseling, and group teachings. I want to thank all those who participated in these teachings, both church members and friends who these teachings were originally prepared for, and who made it possible, that others now can enjoy.

Finally, I want to thank my family for allowing me the time during evenings and weekends so that I could work and finish the manuscript. For my dear wife Terry and for my darling daughter Dolores, I realize it was a sacrifice in order that I could have such gain. Their love and understanding goes beyond what words can describe.

TABLE OF CONTENTS

INTRODUCTION

A role model is a person who exemplifies behavior characteristics, lifestyle, and social or economic status that one admires and chooses to emulate. I would like you to take a moment and reflect on the people you have looked up to as role models. Consider the qualities or circumstances that persuaded you to want to be like them. Now, please eliminate all but the one person you think had the most impact on your life. Do your best to honestly inquire of yourself and provide the best answer for the following questions. Be mindful that these are your private thoughts, and only for your benefit.

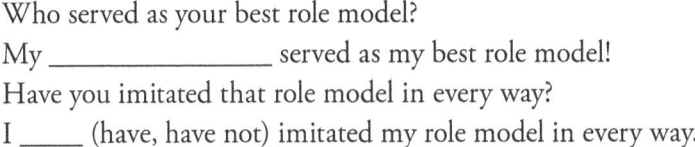

It is very likely that you do not have a perfect role model to imitate in every way. People by nature are each flawed and imperfect in one way or another. Someone may be your role model in a limited way, but no one that you know is the perfect role model. We are given only one example of a perfect role model, and that is the Messiah, Jesus Christ whose example each and every one of us can and should follow. Christ was the example followed by the Apostle Paul, and you can look to Paul as a prototypical role model in his relationships with others to the extent he modeled his behavior after Christ. Paul says in 1 Corinthians 4:16;

> Wherefore I beseech you, be ye
> followers of me. KJV

In the KJV we are called out to follow after the Apostle Paul. If we examine this closer in the NASB version, you see that to follow after is explained as living according to the Gospel, which can be accomplished by imitating the example of how to live one's life as seen in the life of the apostle Paul. We know that Jesus provided the example found in the Gospels, which Paul followed and worked passionately to obey.

> Therefore I exhort you,
> be imitators of me. (NASB)

The Apostle Paul communicates to the Church to, "follow my example". His example is based on the teachings of Jesus in obedience to the Father's will, and according to the revealed Word of God. There are many people who have come across your path, some who might have served as a good role model in limited ways, but only a select few persons can lead us in the steps of Jesus Christ. For the most part, you go at it alone, stumbling through life searching for someone considered worthy of following, in whose steps, in their limited ways might exhibit the righteous and desirable qualities you should emulate. However, you must remain ready to disclaim their leadership when they stray off the righteous path and not fall into the same ditch with the blind.

You have only one perfect example, and that is the Lord Jesus Christ. You need to arrive at the point in your life that you can look only to Jesus and yearn to imitate Him in every way. You must work to rise to the measure of the stature of Christ by patterning your life to be like Jesus and obtain the fullness of Him. (Ephesians 4:13)

This Study is about building up relationships. There have been many books written and seminars conducted that discuss building relationships, but few reflect the Christian biblical perspective. Some works utilized in churches in relationship counseling seminars fall short of the mark, applying secular values which are not aligned with scripture. Although, there are many works that are excellent and, properly applied, they produce positive results in couples counseling and relationship building. We will not be discussing currently popular how-to secular methods for maintaining relationships, but instead, we will turn to the Bible to learn what it says regarding relationships. Then we will study the qualities that are found in the best example of a relationship, Jesus and the Father to the extent we can apply their same principles in our lives. We will explore the foundation principles Jesus used to build relationships with others while He was here on earth. We can agree that His principles worked perfectly for Him, and you will want to understand how these principles are sure to work just as well for you.

The primary relationship we want to consider is the one between Jesus and the Father. Didn't they have the right, perfect and most desirable relationship? Let us review some elements of their relationship:

They did not lie to one another.

John 17:17

Each held nothing back from the other, (except for the time of the end of the world God reserved for Him only to know). "But of that day and hour knoweth no man, no, not the angels of heaven, but My Father only." (Matthew 24:36)

They had full trust in each other and remained open to the other's concerns.

Luke 22:42

Their love was, is, and will be inseparable.

John 17:26

This should be the prototype for the relationship you yearn to have. God offers each of us the opportunity to have similar relationships with others as He has with Jesus. Their relationship is unique and serves as the model for the successful inter-human relationship, which will work best after you have established a relationship with the Father reflective of His prototype. In order for you to have God's type of relationship you must first have your own quality relationship with God. It is also necessary that you establish a relationship of commensurate quality with Jesus, Him as your Lord and you as His bonded servant. Subsequently, you may be able to have relationships of similar quality with others. Whether or not you have a good relationship is strictly up to you. The type of relationship you establish is within your control, and you don't have to stay in a relationship which is unproductive or harmful. You can have a perfect relationship with Jesus, and you can have a perfect relationship with others who you invite to partake in your life, if you fashion it after the prototype given in Jesus' relationship with God.

Greater love hath no man than this, that
a man lay down his life for his friends.

John 15:13

Throughout our study, unless otherwise noted, we will utilize the Authorized King James Version of the Bible (KJV) as the source for scripture references. We will review scripture in other versions for clarity and to bring forth the full modern understanding of the scripture.

In this book you will learn about the basic elements of relationships that are fundamental to every relationship. The Holy Scriptures found only in the Bible, the inimitable Word of God, is the main source utilize for exploring relationships, in this work. We will establish a set of Christian biblical principles from the Bible that are foundational elements essential for building and maintaining relationships. They are titled, the "Higher Ground Principles". These principles are individually explained throughout the book, and collectively listed in the appendix to further enhance the point of rising steps for yourself to climb to reach higher ground.

As a Christian you have been called to live out your life in imitation of the Lord Jesus, according to Christian biblical principles. Therefore, you are obligated to know these principles and to embrace them as the pattern source for your behavior, as you relate to others. This can only be accomplished by applying Biblical principles in the course of daily living. You cannot simply be Christian on Sunday morning, and something else the remainder of the week. Your lifestyle, in its totality, must conform to the lifestyle of the Gospel, even if it requires radical change. As you adopt

Christian biblical principles into your lifestyle, you will immediately see change come into your life. How you view others, and more importantly, how you treat and deal with others will transform into a pleasant and enjoyable experience each and every time.

The second part of the Book continues the exploration of the "Qualities for Christian Living" by examining various critical categories of the Christian's life that pose severe challenges to establishing and sustaining sound relationships. These challenges include the "how-to" on handling conflict with others, offences you are prone to commit and offences committed against you, and conflict within the church. We will also examine what the Word teaches on how your perspective on money impacts your personal financial condition and affects your relationships with others.

We will consider the effect of spiritual laws, how they always work the same for everyone who meets their conditions. You don't have to be a Christian to enjoy the effect of a spiritual law. Spiritual laws, like physical and natural laws have existed since creation. God has handed down detailed explanations to His people throughout time, as seen in the Law of Moses to the Israelites and subsequently throughout the scriptures. These laws work the same all the time for everyone. You can liken it to rain. When it rains, it rains on everyone. The promises of God are spiritual. Certain promises made to Abraham were made while he was yet a Gentile. Abraham is God's designee to be the father of nations two generations before Jacob was born, before the nation Israel was chosen as God's people. Abraham believed God and it was accounted to him for righteousness. (Romans 4:3). Likewise, everyone who believes God will also receive God's promises. *Building Blocks for Relationships* displays godly principles that work equally for the Christian and the non-Christian when applied. My hope is that you will try these principles and apply them in your daily life and, whether Christian or not, enjoy a richer life and a higher quality in your relationships. I trust you to work on having a perfect relationship in your life.

Our study concludes with a review of what constitutes a perfect relationship. It leads us into deeper understanding of how love and forgiveness are the main support for a healthy and vibrant relationship with the ones you choose to spend your life with.

While reading this Book you will find it helpful indeed to keep your personal Bible by your side. Bible quotes appear often, and to amplify your understanding you should go directly to the scripture and harvest for yourself the wonderful truths that it unveils. I prefer the King James Version for myself, but you are free to use the version you are most familiar with. My encouragement is for you to use the Bible in conjunction with your reading.

The design of this work allows for individual reading, or for a group teaching to be conducted for any number of participants. If you would like assistance in how to organize and conduct the teaching or prepare for an event for your family, fellowship, Bible study group or Church, please feel free to contact me, and I will assist you in preparing for the event. I only ask that you read the Book in its entirety before you undertake the responsibility of teaching it to others. May God bless you abundantly, in Christ.

Gaspar

PART

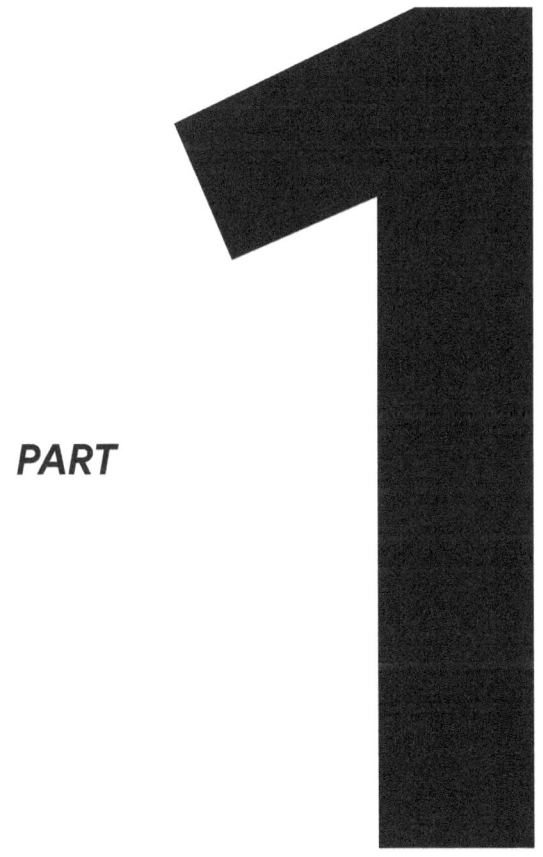

I.

Laying *the* Foundation

Building Blocks for Relationships is a study of the principles in the Bible that set the foundations for constructing relationships. These principles are durable and provide rules that instill and maintain stability in the relationship. They comprise the guide you'll need to building up your relationship, and encourage virtuosity, love, and care in handling your affairs. These principles are indispensable, as you relate with others, and in pursuing the purposes that bring and bind you together with someone else. The study is based on biblical principles that are contained within spiritual laws. Since the principles for building a relationship are based on spiritual laws, when you do what is commanded in the Bible, you will receive the intended godly benefit. The result of your actions will be positive consistently, if you are acting as a believer in Christ, out of faith, and if you are acting from your heart in obedience to the commands from the Holy Scriptures, which is God's Word revealed to man. Because, God is not a respecter of persons you will receive the intended benefit. In the study, we will examine the scriptures for greater understanding of biblical principles with the xpectation that when applied they will actually work.

The biblical field of study on relationships is very broad. While this study and workshop exercises touch on the fundamentals that one applies in a relationship, it does not by any means exhaust the topic. As you begin your new self-assessment of how to relate to others, bear in mind that this, at best, is a work in progress. Likewise, building up your relationship will take much work and will require consistent effort to enable you to claim even the slightest mastery of skill in relationship building. Think positively and afford yourself every opportunity to apply any corrections needed to improve your relationship. Also, this is calling for you to lose your fear of change. In order to obtain the foundations for building good relationships, you will have to change the ways you have been using to the ways revealed in the Word. One of the most important acts on your part is to remove pride from your behavior motivation, and to think of your existing relationships as works in progress that need much attention, repairs, and time for healing. If you apply the new tools found in this book when creating a new relationship, you will be surprised to find that you have become a master at building the best relationships.

The book of Ecclesiastes teaches on the necessity for man to have relationships. Either we cooperate together to build on a successful endeavor, or we compete to outdo each other. When you depend solely on yourself, you cannot see from other vantage points with clarity. You are depending on your intellect, skill or prowess to champion you across the finish line first. But collaboration with others is like adding the colors of the rainbow to a canvas that was otherwise black and white or grey. A partnership is a collaboration to achieve some mutual purpose or goal, and it creates a natural environment for the relationship that ensues. In this partnership relationship varying and different ideas can emerge and greater depth can be achieved. The advantage clearly falls to the side of cooperation, of having a healthy and prosperous relationship. (Ecclesiastes 4:9-13).

> I have seen that every labor and every
> skill which is done is the result of rivalry
> between a man and his neighbor. This
> too is vanity and striving after wind.

Ecclesiastes 4:4 NASB

While it takes at least two people to establish a relationship, the only one you can exercise absolute control over is yourself. A relationship is not built on controlling the actions of others, but on the degree and ability you possess over your own self, which is self-control. There is no doubt that your partner is not perfect, as the only perfect human was Jesus, but it is not incumbent upon you to fix that person by controlling them in order to have a good relationship. That spells disaster to the relationship either now or later. No one enjoys being controlled by another. They may put up with it for a while to get what they want out of the relationship, but the effect is not genuine and won't be long lasting, they are manipulating you into thinking that you have control.

Self-control is the sole guide one must adhere to in their behavior. Most of us practice control over other people in one form or another. Some have mastered the skill which is often masked in some form of desirable behavior like being extra cute, seeming to possess above average intelligence, being a big spender, tough or harsh, just to name a few. Whatever your choice for exercising control over others, it will lead to conflict, frustration, and, if there is anything worse, you may experience that as well. You must begin by deliberately breaking the cycle in your life of wanting to control others, and you must start to exercise self-control. This will instantly improve your relationship and increase the potential for better relationships in the future.

The study will not equip you with the secular skills and techniques for maintaining a relationship. Surely, there is a place for their application as well. However, this study focuses on building the biblical foundations for the construct of a godly relationship. Let us begin by understanding that according to God's Word (1 Corinthians 4:4-5) we are forbidden to judge others. You should not stand in judgment of another's level of spirituality or the amount of Word knowledge your partner may or may not have. Instead, concentrate on your own abilities so that you may rise up to be the spiritual leader and lead by example in building up your relationship. It will require much sacrifice on your part, (the sacrifice of restraining yourself) and you should be prepared to sacrifice everything available to you in order to maintain the biblical precepts required in a godly relationship.

II.

Have T.H.I.S. *in* Your Relationship

HIGHER GROUND PRINCIPLE # 1

Establish relationships on the principles taught in the Bible.

To fulfill its purpose, a relationship must be healthy, prosperous, and robust. It must be regularly groomed and fed with proper nutrition to prevent sickness, disease, and death. The base elements in the foundation of a healthy relationship are **Truth, Honesty, Integrity, and Sincerity (THIS).** Without THIS in its proper place and in effect, efforts to perfect a relationship will fall short. Every good relationship needs to have God as the third string to bind it, and our spiritual God dwells in the center of these four qualities.

The ultimate desire is to have transparency in the relationship. Unless there is a full commitment from the parties in the relationship to be one hundred percent truthful, honest, sincere, and act with integrity at all times, the relationship will experience opaque spotting and obscured accounting of events that affect and cast negative reflections on the relationship. To have clarity at all times and to achieve transparency in the relationship, it must have THIS in operation in the heart of each partner.

TRUTH

Truth is correct knowledge or doctrine. It is the lowest common denominator for knowledge or information, whose material substance cannot be changed.

Truth is fidelity (the quality or state of being faithful), constancy (freedom from change).

A truth is always the same and works the same all the time, every time, without exception. For example, gravity is a truth. Whenever an object is dropped, it will always fall to the ground. No matter how many times you try this, it will always work the same way. This is known as a law of physics (*physical laws*). There are laws of nature (*natural laws*) that yield a specified result when certain conditions are met, such as planting a seed in order for it to grow into a plant. There are also laws of men (*man-made laws*) that are generally weak and inconsistent, because they are subjective and governed by varying circumstances and emotional persuasions.

There are also spiritual truths, or principles in the Bible, that act as *spiritual laws*. When applied, these truths consistently produce a predictable result. These spiritual laws are put into operation when we act upon what we believe, or better said, when we act on our faith. "A soft answer turneth away wrath" (Proverbs 15:1). It works every time.

Knowing and believing that Jesus is the Son of God makes you free from dogmas and untrue worship. Jesus is the way, and He always leads us to the truth via the true worship of God. Others that we might follow lack the quality of absolute truth and can and will lead us away from true worship.

There is deceitfulness from others, institutions, and governments, and there is also deceitfulness that comes from within oneself. The hardest to overcome, of course, is self-deceit. Self-deceit leads you away from true worship of God into worshipping other things with the expectation that these other things will do for you what God promises, is willing, and is able to perform. Self-deceit is among the biggest un-truths that plague mankind and that affects having a basic relationship with God, and which consequently affects your relationship with others.

Who changed the truth of God into
a lie, and worshipped and served the
creature more than the Creator, who is
blessed for ever. Amen.

Romans 1:25

Changing the truth, which is a euphemism for lying, causes encasement and imprisonment, and removes freedom from our daily lives. We become encased, and our hearts become encrusted. This is a spiritual law at work. This is why you feel so bad and uneasy after telling a lie. When you lie it creates a condition that leaves you heavily laden with guilt brought about by sin. The burden of the lie weighs heavily on you and everything you do, especially when those to whom you have lied are nearby. That causes unnecessary social strain and is an impediment to having an improved relationship.

Let no corrupt communication proceed
out of your mouth, but that which is
good to the use of edifying, that it may
minister grace unto the hearers.

Ephesians 4:29

But speaking the truth in love, may
grow up into him in all things, which is
the head, even Christ:

Ephesians 4:15

Love rejoices in the truth. Living in truth keeps you filled with joy and leaves no room for remorse.

If you want joy in your relationship, then you should build the relationship on truth. You may desire to improve your relationship, and this will take some effort and hard work on your part. To begin a new relationship or to rejuvenate a decaying one, you must speak and live the truth. You should do a self-assessment of what you've yet to completely reveal about yourself in order to come clean to your partner. It took the boldness of the prophet Nathan (2 Samuel 12) to help King David realize how far he had removed himself from God by avoiding the truth about his sin of adultery with Bathsheba. A sin that was further complicated by adding the sin of ordering Bathsheba's husband Uriah be sent to the front lines to be killed. This was an act of murder, in that he instructed the taking of an innocent life, and that of the life of one of his mighty men, loyal friend, and a soldier in battle willing to die for David's kingdom This did David so that he could keep his lie hidden from his other mighty men and the nation. However, there are no secrets from God, and trying to keep one is the biggest breach of the truth a person can commit. If there are lies you are keeping in order to hold on to your relationship, you are only making it worse.

You have to gird up your loins (by going to the Word), build up your courage, and have a heart-to-heart conversation with your partner. God defines truth in Jesus, and Jesus is your best role model for building a relationship on truth. Remember that men should not judge one another, because we are each guilty of the same things. You tend to not see your own faulty behavior, as when you fail to see the beam sticking out your eye, but are quick to find the splinter, the fault in others, for the same things you are trying to get away with. You will find that as you come together around the truth, it will diminish the passion to sit in judgement of others. (Luke 6:41-42).

Truth without judgment sets you free and is the fountain of rejoicing which waters the relationship and keeps it in bloom. You find truth in the Messiah, Jesus Christ, and are strongly urged to dress in truth as part of your armor, the armor of God given through the Lord Jesus Christ.

Stand therefore, having fastened on the
belt of truth…

Ephesians 6:14 (ESV)

The belt of truth spoken of here surrounds and supports your loins. It is referring to the soft belly and the under-belly part of the body. This section is very vulnerable, the organs inside are more exposed in comparison to the chest plate guarding your heart and lungs. This is a perfect analogy for understanding how vulnerable you are when it comes to keeping the the truth. Absence of the truth leaves you wide open to exposure from many sides, and you want to have all your sides protected. Lying can become the comfortable choice. But lying is not the better choice. Lying makes a compelling argument to the natural, old-man senses for you looking better in a given situation. But in the spiritual realm, the truth is set in stone, as by the spirit it will set you free from the bondage and other baggage that comes with lying. Lying causes unnecessary bondage, and bondage is extremely harmful to the relationship, for it causes things to remain opaque rather than things being clear between you and your partner.

HONESTY

HIGHER GROUND PRINCIPLE # 2

Have honest behavior and integrity, and be sincere in everything you do.

Now that we have an understanding of the importance truth bears on the success of the relationship, let us move on and closely examine another component of the four pillars in the foundation of a sound and healthy relationship: honesty.

Honesty is fairness and straightforwardness of conduct exemplified in every aspect of the relationship while dealing in truth. (Exodus 23: 1-9) Honesty does not waiver. It is like a cargo ship heading to its destination through fair weather and through storms; its course is not altered.

Honesty is best defined as always being truthful. Honesty is essential to building up a relationship, and is used as the tool for measuring veracity in what is said. Honesty applies to things said, and by extension, it applies to behavior as well. "Actions speak louder than words" is a very popular saying, and it carries a lot of weight in the context of behaving honestly. A person may speak words that are true, but their actions, gestures, posture, and facial expression may convey a meaning incongruous with the spoken message. This is deceptive and dishonest when it does not represent the entire truth. It is dishonest to paint the truth in your favor, or to leave out pertinent facts that might be revealing or convicting, otherwise.

In the work environment, for example, a married woman might have a conversation with a male co-worker who invites her out for drinks. She may say, "Oh, but you know I'm married," in a manner that encourages continuing the conversation. Perhaps she gives a look or positions her body in an inviting way that conflicts with her statement of unavailability due to marriage. Although she told the truth about being married, she failed the test of honesty.

An honest relationship has boundaries that are clear and discernable. These boundaries must be established at the beginning of the relationship, and concerning on-going broken relationships, repairs can only be achieved through honest effort and commitment on the part of both parties. In an honest relationship, the intent of the relationship is well defined and distinctly understood by each partner. The conversation between the co-workers should spell out that they can be friends, and if they meet after work for social purposes, they should be joined by their spouses. The relationship is thereby, defined as a friendship, and classified as to how they will relate to each other going forward. It keeps intentions transparent, and their relationship evolves into a family friendship.

In the relationship, you should not address one another in misleading or dishonest ways. Honesty leads to godliness and is God-like in every way. Honesty has no variableness, it is always consistent, and engenders an atmosphere of reliability in each other. If your intentions are honest from the beginning, you would extricate yourself from situations where lust or covetousness provoke you into participating illicitly outside of the relationship, which may bring shame, or cause a break-up of what might have otherwise been the perfect beneficial relationship. You must overcome every carnal force that attacks the relationship by rejecting to go along with ungodly and lustful temptations, and choose to live your life soberly and strengthened against temptations. (Titus 2:11-12). When you have been honest consistently, you will inspire confidence from those around you and especially from your partner. Your partner, mate, spouse, child, friend, or employee can take refuge in knowing that a safe and predictable environment exists in every encounter with you. You, on the other hand, will experience living in openness, truth, and enjoy having peace and joy when relating with the ones you choose to be with.

Honesty builds trust. A good example of this trust is found in 2 Kings 12:15. I will quote from the NASB because the language in this verse of scripture is made clearer to our modern-day understanding.

> Moreover, they did not require an
> accounting from the men into whose
> hand they gave the money to pay to
> those who did the work,
> for they dealt faithfully.

The men administering the funds to pay the laborers repairing the temple received donations and contributions, but no one felt it necessary to keep or require any accounting from them because they had a reputation for honesty and were well renowned throughout their community as upstanding men. No one doubted that they did exactly what was required, and that they would perform what was expected of them. Honesty goes a long way in any relationship by removing the burdens brought on by guilt and doubt.

Honesty is fundamental to strengthening your relationship. When you deal honestly with your partner, there will be no aura of doubt or slack in the trust factor regarding you. Your actions and judgments will be acceptable all the time. Your partner will be assured that your motives and purposes are derived from honest intentions for the betterment of the relationship, and free of unselfish drives, since they have known you only to be honest at all times.

Dishonesty carries a heavy burden and usually ends in pain and suffering for either partner, or most likely for both. A break-up is hard and painful on everyone involved. There are consequences for dishonesty, even if they don't seem apparent at the time of the incident. Elisha the prophet had a servant, sort of a right-hand man, named Gehazi. Elisha was an honest man and wanted nothing but what God provided for him, and all that he did was for God's glory. His servant Gehazi was not honest to speak of, and he was greedy. Unwilling to see the riches that Elisha rejected pass him by, Gehazi defied his master's orders. He lied about what he did, and hid the goods he illicitly obtained from the Syrian General, who unwittingly, though very gladly gave Gehazi all he asked for, believing it was by Elisha's request as payment for being healed of leprosy. God sees it all and He chose to reveal Gehazi's dishonesty to Elisha. For his dishonesty, greed and disobedience, Gehazi received the gift from above of leprosy for him and all his descendants forever. Always remember that there are consequences to not being honest. You never know just how extensive the consequences will be. (2 Kings 5:20-27).

INTEGRITY

As you increase in appreciation for the foundational principles of truth and honesty, your understanding will continue expanding to greater heights. Other principles like integrity when placed alongside will further enhance knowledge of how these elements work together to bring joy and fulfillment when spending time with others.

Just as the elements of truth and honesty are necessary components for forming the sound foundation to the relationship, integrity is also essential to building a solid foundation for your relationship to rest upon for years to come. Different than truth and honesty, integrity provides assurance that a partner can be relied upon, that he will uphold and measure up to the godly principles that strengthen the relationship. Integrity assured that the other party in the relationship is willing to perform their righteous duties at all times, and especially when required. If one party strays off course and needs correction, they will be receptive to the advice and encouragement from the partner, as the other compassionately offers guidance and assistance free of accusation, judgement or persecution, and absent of selfish gain, to assure that truth and honesty are upheld. Integrity allows the partners to have open confrontations and air out faults with a willingness to accept to do the right and beneficial thing, as should've been done in the first place.

Integrity is the state of being complete or undivided, exercising righteousness without wavering.

I will behave myself wisely in a perfect
way. O when wilt thou come unto
me? I will walk within my house with
a perfect heart. I will set no wicked
thing before mine eyes: I hate the
work of them that turn aside; it shall
not cleave to me.

Psalms 101:2—3

Integrity is the manifestation of wise behavior that originates in your heart, the part of your mind that is the seat of your convictions. A person of integrity understands the principles in God's Word and does not waiver from them in the slightest way, and if he does, because of his integrity he will return to the right path and accept the consequences. It is easy to yield to fleshly desires, which as the Word tells us are always in opposition to God's ways. Worldly desires consist of pride, greed, lust, avarice, etc., which open the door of temptation to lying, cheating or withholding the truth. In order to resist such temptations, you must be prepared in advance by incorporating methods of passive resistance into your behavior pattern. Let's say a family member has a tendency to say or do things that really irk you. Now, you can wait until they come at you again and react accordingly, or you can prepare yourself in advance to resist the temptation to respond in kind. You will uphold your integrity by keeping to the biblical principles, such as loving your enemy, even though he is not literally your enemy, but at the moment, your feelings could cause you to treat him like one.

We find that integrity itself is founded on four principles:

1. Wisely chosen behavior that is accepted by others.
2. Having purity about your ways, beginning and emanating at home, but carried out throughout your daily walk and conversation, as a qualitative feature in you for others to see.
3. Not seeking or finding pleasure in ungodly and wicked behavior, nor engaging in impure things, no matter how politically correct

they may seem or how many others around you are behaving in that ungodly way.

4. Not allowing the ungodly works of others to enter or stay in your mind, and not harboring destructive images or thoughts in your mind, but instead, being empty of these thoughts and remaining open to the Lord with a clean mind.

In your relationships, identifying integrity will appear to be more abstract than singling out truth and honesty. Truth can be easily discerned, and if you get away with a lie, it may not be long before the truth comes out. Honesty is immediately noticeable in your behavior, and guilt will haunt the believer when he or she has been dishonest. Your partner will most likely know that you are not acting honestly from the onset. You have certain tells, signs and patterns that your partner knows about you which easily betray your attempt to deceive. However, although lack of integrity leaves room for doubt and time for the culprit to come up with a novel explanation, in a relationship, lack of integrity is a formula for disaster. Your partner may get a whiff right away that something is not quite up to snuff, and may choose to file it away for future reference, or save it as ammunition for the next encounter. At this point, you will be under their watch and likely to get caught red-handed at your next slipup. Avoid the risk. If you truly value the relationship and want it to thrive, then have integrity in your dealings.

Many friendships, marriages and other relationships are destroyed for lack of integrity on one or both partners' part. These instances of unspoken issues, over time, are the catalysts which spark future disagreements because they remained unspoken until the final straw that breaks the camel's back. Later in a disagreement it becomes the center of explosive debate in place of a mutual, respectful disagreement. It is more difficult for the relationship to recover from an explosive confrontation that causes deep wounds, than from a mutual disagreement where integrity has not come into question. Women, in general, tend to have better memories of incidents surrounding lack of integrity in their partners than men, because they possess a higher, keener awareness. To men, it comes across as a phenomenon they can't master, and men usually complain that women always bring up the past in a fight. This may seem unfair to the person being accused, but usually it's his or her lack of integrity that has brought things to a boil.

The solution may seem simplistic. "Let each one of you speak the truth with his neighbor…", says Ephesians 4:25. For the culprit, it's very difficult to implement a sudden change in attitude and behavior, as this has been a life pattern incorporated for his survival. The one thing that brought about this kind of change in me was the woman I truly loved, and was not willing to risk losing due to the entrenched negative behavior I had built up over my lifetime. I realized that if I wanted to enjoy my dream relationship, I had to overcome even the deepest negative patterns in my life. The simple answer is to have integrity. To have integrity means that you are a truthful person and everything you do is of honest purpose and intent.

Chapter 4 of the Book of Ephesians is highly instructional to the believer who wants to learn and practice biblical principals relevant to this topic. Ephesians 4:14 speaks to no longer being children tossed to and fro. Ephesians 4:15 directs us to speak the truth. The remainder of the chapter encourages change from what we are to becoming men and women of renewed minds. The latter part of the chapter from verses 21 to 32 reminds us that Jesus is our standard for truth, and it instructs us on the basics for living in true righteousness and holiness. It tells us to stop acting the way we used to act in our "old man" days which were "corrupt according to deceitful lusts".

Integrity bears the charge to put away lying, to not harbor anger, to not take what is not yours. Entering into an illicit relationship is stealing from your spouse, and stealing from the other person's time and emotions that are ill placed. When reality strikes, it will bring to everyone connected severe recovery pains, should recovery be still possible. Integrity also bears the charge not to speak words that tear others down. Instead of speaking corruptly about others, we are to speak only things that build others up, and to perform such other things as being kind, tenderhearted, and forgiving. Integrity will dwell in you when you have internalized these principles in the depth of your convictions, so that when confronted with an unsavory situation you will not think from an evil reference, but you will speak and deal from a godly reference.

If you want your relationship to flourish without strife and conflict, integrity is the element to work on in your life.

Integrity was integral to the relationship of David and Jonathan, as we can see in 1 Samuel 20. David and Jonathan took vows that even though King Saul, Jonathan's father, was attempting to take David's life, Jonathan would remain his loyal friend despite his father treating Jonathan in a rough way. His integrity to his vow saved David's life. It would've been easy and right for Jonathan to obey his father in the commission of King Saul's wrongful act, but his vow to his friend was stronger, and Jonathan's integrity persevered.

SINCERITY

Sincerity is abstract and difficult to identify right away in someone's behavior. You have to get to know a person in order to see that he can be insincere. Sincerity can be masked with varying degrees of deception. You can do something that is seemingly good for your partner, but have the wrong motivation for doing it. Or you could say something that sounds nice in your partner's ears, but not really mean it. What you are saying is what you think your partner wants to hear. The motivation could be to avoid an argument or to hide the truth, but regardless the motivation for being insincere in your relationship, there will be consequences. Hypocrisy is the by-product of insincerity. Hypocrisy will exist in one form or another when intentions are not clear and upright, or used to gain a benefit by manipulating your partner. Let's recall what the Lord Jesus thought about the hypocrisy of the Pharisees. He commented that they pretended to be obedient to the Law of Moses, but to only appear holy for public display. In private, they did whatever they pleased, often contrary to the Law. Those Jews, the ones that were called hypocrites by the Lord, did not have a very good relationship with Jesus. In fact, John the Baptist, apart from Jesus, referred to them as a generation of vipers. They were insincere and wished only that they be thought of as holy, and to be held in high esteem, but it was solely for the purpose of having things their way. The warning was to do as they say, because they were quoting from the Law, but to not imitate what they did, because they were insincere hypocrites. (Matthew 6:2).

Ask yourself, "Am I doing insincere things in my relationship? Am I being a hypocrite because I only want to be viewed as a good person rather than, in actuality being a good person? Do I give the appearance of doing God's Word, but only pretending to appear as a righteous person, loyal and truthful?" This is an inherent problem in many relationships, that is carried over from previous bad habits then introduced into the new relationship without taking into account the bad effect it can have on your partner's perception of you, and that it will negatively impact the relationship in due time. It merits paying close attention to the issue of sincerity or lack of sincerity in your life.

Sincerity is the personal quality of living life from a pure motive without deceit, always being genuine and deliberate in your actions.

> Now this is our boast: Our conscience
> testifies that we have conducted
> ourselves in the world, and especially in
> our relations with you, in the holiness
> and sincerity that are from God. We
> have done so not according to worldly
> wisdom but according to God's grace.

2 Corinthians 1:12; NIV

Sincerity does not allow room for your thoughts about others to be tainted with evil for personal gain or to deal hypocritically with someone else to gain popularity or maintain favor or friendship. Sincerity is always doing what is right, fair, and unquestionably correct. Truth and honesty are the starting point if you aspire to be sincere. A deliberate effort is needed on your part to build integrity into every aspect of your life. As you engage with your partner, you should shed any desire to do things that are motivated by disingenuous intentions and that will impede achieving godly purposes in your relationship. Your partner will know and trust your every action and respect your every decision when you are perceived as being sincere. In a relationship, integrity generates trustworthiness, because the parties know that each one's actions are based on truth and for truth's sake. Integrity makes you reliable and a stand-up guy in your partner's eyes.

Should you find yourself in doubt whether you are acting sincerely or not, try applying this process to your thinking; I call it **"FRB"**. It stands for doing what is **Fair**, what is **Right** and what is **Best**. The results from FRB will always be a win-win situation for all parties. When you do what is fair, it will stand scrutiny, and what is right cannot be denied, and what is best defines the best outcome (win/win) for all.

When there has been an obvious breach in integrity it is incumbent upon the "villain" to promptly move to repair the breach and restore himself or herself with their partner. A relationship should be built on firm and solid foundations to withstand external and internal assaults due to human frailties that can lead to a schism or destruction in the relationship. Should a breach occur in the relationship you must move quickly to mend it, and the aggrieved partner must reach deep into their soul to find mercy, employ the love of God within them and activate brotherly love in the situation at hand. Forgiveness should not be looked upon as a "get out jail free card", or as a God given right to be claimed by the culprit. It is a requirement of the aggrieved to carry forth God's grace for their own sake in maintaining unobstructed fellowship with the Lord. The offender must repent and reconcile to stay in right fellowship with the Lord. This response is encouraged through honest, forthcoming commitment to take immediate action to stem the partner's emotional bleeding. A breach of integrity must be remedied immediately by divulging the cause and circumstance that brought stimulated the incident, and to examine if there are root causes that need to be addressed. Many relationships have been severely damaged from innocent behavior in a bad situation, or from bad behavior. The cause must be assessed and treated by both parties, and if needed, to solicit the aid of a competent third-party mediator, counselor or Pastor, if an objective third party's participation is sought.

The four pillars that rise from the foundation to solidly support the relationship are comprised of THIS. Truth, honesty, integrity and sincerity are essential for a godly and successful relationship.

ALWAYS IN REMEMBRANCE (2 PETER 1:15)

1. Relationship pertains to our affairs and _____ with others.
2. We can exercise total _____ over our own actions.
3. Godly relationships are built on _____.
4. Truth is _____ knowledge or doctrine.
5. Laws describe things that _____ the same all the time: physical laws, natural laws, and spiritual laws. Man-made laws are weak because they are not founded on absolute _____
6. Spiritual laws are operated by _____ and by actions corresponding to one's beliefs.
7. Truth shall make you free is a _____ law.
8. Any alteration of the truth is _____.
9. Only God can _____ in truth.
10. When we live in truth, our lives are full of _____.
11. Honesty is the product of one's conduct when dealing in _____.
12. Integrity is the state of being _____ and undivided in one's behavior.
13. Behavior that is of wise _____ is an aspect of integrity.
14. Purity in one's ways is an aspect of _____.
15. _____ is required when faced with temptation.
16. Not holding _____ thoughts in one's mind reflects integrity in one's character.
17. Living life with pure motives and without _____ is a quality of sincerity.
18. Thoughts tainted with _____ or hypocrisy are not founded on sincerity.

SCRIPTURE REFERENCE:

Ephesians 4:15, 29; Exodus 23:1-9 Psalms 101:2-3; 2 Corinthians 1:12; Titus 2:11-12;

2 Kings 12:15; Ephesians 4:14; Matthew 6:2; Ephesians 4:21-32; 2 Kings 5:20-27;

Ephesians 6:14; Luke 6:41-42; Ephesians 4:29; Romans 1:25; Proverbs 15:1;

Ecclesiastes 4:4; Ecclesiastes 9:13

III.

WHAT CONSTITUTES *a* RELATIONSHIP?

HIGHER GROUND PRINCIPLE # 3

Identify the biblical qualities you want in your relationship.

A relationship is a state of affairs existing between those dealing with others.

A relationship exists between two or more persons who have a purpose in common such as, husband/wife, doctor/patient, parent/child, teacher/student, employer/employee, and friend/friend.

A relationship is entered into for the good of the participants, partners, or associates to benefit from a common or symbiotic undertaking requiring interaction for achieving beneficial goals. The parties in a relationship can choose to cooperate by sharing information, partnering skills and talents, or agreeing to nurture and support one another. When motives are clear, the parties to the relationship may offer up their contribution without expecting an equal portion or value in return. Our modern culture emphasizes a fifty-fifty contribution from husband and wife and equal participation in the marriage. This is a faulty premise that puts emphasis on measuring imbalance in the relationship and opens the door to mistrust and leads to conflict and distress, as there are so many variables that cannot be measured or bear emotional impact in a marriage. The same principles apply in other relationships, as well. A homemaker and mother may not feel as important as the executive or professional husband enjoying his daily practice, but she cannot measure how important it is for her husband to know that she is caring for the home and children, which he would prefer not to entrust to anyone else. The basis for measuring the contribution and participation is skewed from the other person's point of view when trying to measure their value to the relationship. There is a tendency to think that your contribution is the most important, or at least the one that requires the most work. It is important to be aware of the value or worth you bring to the relationship, and also to weigh the value of what your partner brings to the relationship, and if both are contributing the max. Then there is the concern of how your partner perceives your value, and whether it's important to the relationship for it to be quantified. If there is a benefit to be had; i.e.: it brings you closer together, establishes equity of contribution, or establishes a sense of fair play, then it may be worthwhile pursuing what is the overall perception of each one's value and contribution to the relationship.

Homemakers obliged to stay home and raise the children while the spouse goes to work may have been severely hurt by even the thought that her husband is straying. But the relationship can be hurt by either spouse straying into the arms of another person outside their own relationship, or due to one or the other simply feeling overworked and undervalued. The working spouse provider may stray, but they too may be hurt to learn that the homemaker has been distracted from providing the utmost care for the children and the home for a self-redeeming adventure outside the husband/wife relationship. Either or both of these problems can be made to go away before they occur by applying the concepts we have learned about truth, honesty, integrity and sincerity, (THIS). You may take inventory of where you are in your relationship and why you are in that place, remembering that you can exercise control over yourself, but your partner has to be educated and led to the level you are at so that they too may be made aware of the need to exercise control over themselves. Consider the following questions and truthfully answer them in your heart. When you have formed your answers, I strongly recommend that you discuss them openly with your partner, and be objectively receptive to any feedback you receive, whether you agree with it or not.

What do you want out of your relationship?

What were you seeking when you decided to enter into this relationship? For example, did you enter the relationship because you wanted to share your love or because you craved to be loved?

Were your motives clear, and did you have agreement of how the value and worth of contributions to the relationship would be measured, was this important at all?

In formulating your answers to the above questions, you may want to consider the following points about relationships:

The basis on which you established the relationship dictates the acceptable terms and conditions for that relationship. Re-examine your purpose and the reason for being in the relationship.

A godly person enters a relationship with a clean heart and seeks to have a clean life in the relationship. The relationship must in some way glorify the Lord.

An unselfish relationship will be founded on THIS (Truth, Honesty, Integrity, and Sincerity).

The worldly person enters a relationship only for personal gain.

A selfish relationship is formed for personal satisfaction and for personal gain.

Lusting after someone and building a relationship purely on physical, sexual desire becomes an unsustainable relationship as conditions change, and personal interests conflict, or desires wane. It is a temporary relationship that will cause pain and discomfort if not acknowledged that it is for short-term convenience and personal satisfaction that cannot last unless it evolves into something else.

In some special way, the person in your relationship is a reflection of you. In Acts 5:1-11, Ananias and Sapphira, a husband and wife, conspired in their relationship to lie to, deceive, and shortchange God from what they promised. They violated the spiritual law of truth. Either one could have prevented the other from committing the lie and averting the untimely loss of both their lives. However, their marriage had devolved into a deteriorated level of greed that excluded having trust in God to supply their every need, and so they took it upon themselves to neglect their faith in God to provide for all their needs.

Entering a relationship, or staying in a relationship for the wrong reasons will gradually cause decay and be the cause of the demise of the relationship. In the case of Ananias and Sapphira it cost them their lives. The purpose you choose to form a relationship should not detract from the potential for growth and health as the relationship matures. A relationship for an illicit purpose will conclude in failure, guilt, or worse.

For example, a relationship formed with your doctor to cheat the insurance company, or your accountant to cheat the IRS, or another person for illicit sex, are all founded on being dishonest and ultimately contribute to the destruction of the relationship, resulting in degradation of your personal values. If you don't work to restore your value, then you as a person will become more difficult to have a relationship with in the future because your base of operation for forming a relationship will be habitually dishonest.

Adultery is very high on the list of acts that are not only sinful, but that also break down your character. Adultery is a selfish behavior and issues out hurt to everyone affected, spouses, children, extended family, the church community, friends, and even the workplace. It is among the worse moral pandemics the world continues to suffer from. Adhering to the principles in the Word of God is the best inoculation from sin, and especially from adultery.

Suggestions for Overcoming Past Experiences:

Don't try to fix what went wrong in the past. You will tend to rely on a knee jerk reaction that doesn't reach down into the root causes of what went wrong or why. Instead, begin right away to do what is right—today, right now—and continue to do the right thing from now on. Begin to live a superior quality of life in your relationship that embraces THIS and has compassion and consideration for your partner and others that may be affected through your relationship, such as children, family, close friends, and of course, the church. In the next chapter, we will study five essential biblical precepts that are necessary to the success of your relationship. It is important for you to understand how each one works and that they are applied throughout your daily interactions. With God, things work rapidly, so you may find that employing His principles into your actions and behaving accordingly will bear instant gratification.

And having in a readiness to revenge
all disobedience, when your obedience
is fulfilled.

2 Corinthians 10:6

ALWAYS IN REMEMBRANCE (2 PETER 1:15)

1. Dealings with _____ constitute the basis for a relationship.
2. Relationships exist between persons who have a _____ in common.
3. We should _____ our purpose before forming a relationship.
4. The _____ for forming a relationship may strongly influence terms and conditions that govern the relationship.
5. A godly person enters a relationship with a _____ heart.
6. Unselfish relationships are founded on THIS: _____, _____, _____, and _____.
7. A worldly person enters a relationship for personal _____.
8. You should work in the relationship to do what is biblically right starting _____.
9. A relationship for an illicit purpose will conclude in _____, guilt, or worse.
10. The terms and conditions of your relationship should reflect a _____ benefit.

SCRIPTURE REFERENCE:

Acts 5: 1—11; 2 Corinthians 10:6

Fundamentals *for* Maintaining *a* Relationships

HIGHER GROUND PRINCIPLE # 4

Work at your relationship for success.

What causes a relationship to work?

THE FIVE SS'

There may be a benefit to studying failed relationships to determine why they failed. A relationship that is decaying can likewise be evaluated. This clinical approach is not novel, but after much protracted study has not yielded a conclusive solution for avoiding failure. Couples counseling is a practical fall back to finding solutions that typically end up in long stupors of complacency, unhappiness and eventual failure on one level or another. Too much time has been spent analyzing faults, placing blame, and making excuses why the relationship is not working. Little has been gained that can be applied to help relationships succeed. Your concern should not be why the relationship failed, but rather, being forward looking by seeking methods to apply based on principles that have worked consistently and are assured to work for you. These would be principles that are sustainable and work to avoid failure. I was inspired to reflect on Jesus' relationship building and maintenance skills, and to glean from His example the things that worked so well for Him, and how they might apply in our lives regarding building and maintaining successful relationships.

In His relationships, Jesus made a full commitment and required the same of those who entered into relationship with Him. His basis was founded on THIS, and those who engaged with commitment received empowerment and self-confidence, as well as the satisfaction of having a relationship with Him. An example of this is seen with the seventy disciples who went out to minister with great confidence and boldness, casting out demons healing the sick, that even the devil fell from heaven. (Luke 10:17-18). There is an example given of the man born blind (John 9:27), after he built a relationship with Jesus, he confronts the Pharisees with extreme boldness and says, "Do you also want to become His disciples". These guys were the religious authorities of the time and no one would dare address them with such a condescending tone. They did not permit anyone to speak to them that way. Ultimately, they excommunicated the formerly blind man from the temple, but they could not remove the new found boldness in him. This phenomenon worked repeatedly whenever Jesus interacted with others who embraced Him in THIS, and it is carried forward by the power of the Holy Spirit as seen in the acts of the Apostles, and in believers going forward since then, even to today.

I am introducing five fundamentals Jesus used in handling His relationships. These principles were present as He established relationships with others. The biblical records bear out the veracity of their application by the Lord, and if applied by you, they will likewise, assure success in every relationship you enter into. Each one of these is a spiritual principle Christ applied while in the flesh, and they are foundational for a relationship with Him in spirit, as well. You too can use these five fundamentals to establish lasting relationships with others. In His daily walk Jesus gives us living examples of proper behavior toward others, and confirms the truth of His principles in His ultimate sacrifice by dying for us on the cross. His central theme was to walk in love, and He asked that we love our enemies as we love ourselves; a fundamental central to relationships with others. These principles each stands alone but together they complete the whole of the substance that drives the relationship and steers it in its proper course. If your relationship were a luxury car THIS would be the four wheels it rolls on, and these five principles (the **Five SS'**) would be the inner workings that make it go; the transmission, engine and other working parts. They are:

Sanctification –	setting the relationship apart
Sacrifice –	giving up something of great value for mutual gain
Substitution –	taking the place for someone else

Submission –	giving in to a different point of view
Survival –	perseverance of the relationship through difficulties

Sanctification: Sets the parties aside or apart from the rest of the world at special moments and for special purposes. Keep your relationship personal and private, not public. Open the doors and allow in only those who support, and who can be beneficial to the success of your relationship.

> Wherefore Jesus also, that he might
> sanctify the people with his own blood,
> suffered without the gate.

Hebrews 13:12

A relationship that is not sanctified (set apart) has its laundry aired everywhere. The wife shares stories of bedroom activities with her friends when they have no business knowing about what goes on behind the couple's closed doors. The husband constantly complains to his friends of how bad a housekeeper his wife is, or that she is spendthrift, and so on. It should never be the case where outsiders are brought into the relationship that has set you apart from them in the first place. What happens in the relationship should stay in that relationship, unless there is imminent physical harm to be concerned about, and if necessary, regarding other matters, both parties should seek and commit to obtaining professional help from a qualified third party.

Exposing inner secrets to outsiders further compounds issues of the relationship by commission of two additional errors. The first error is a accepting a false sense of relief; that you have relieved your anxiety concerning the situation and are being relieved by letting off steam about your partner. The second error is the delusion that you are dishing out well deserved justice on your partner by diminishing his image and tarnishing his reputation in the eyes of your friends. You may be thinking, "My friends finally know who he really is". It gives you the sense of self-imposed justice, that you are finally taking a victory lap and walking away with the trophy, that this makes you the better person, or so you'd like to think.

What truly occurs in this situation is that your friends now think rather poorly of your partner, and consequently, by extension they either pity you, or think that you're not too bright for having made such a poor choice, and then sticking with it throughout the ordeal. If it's about marriage, your friends would have you divorced and collecting alimony in no time. But relationships are more complicated than that, that's why they are set apart. Issues are to be identified and openly discussed between the parties, if an equitable solution is to be found. It is not simple. What if you haven't told your partner what you think about him or her, or you failed to mention how you felt about the particular situation you described to your friends? You told everyone else, but you haven't told him. Where does that leave you? In order to keep your relationship sanctified you must implement true and real solutions to problems as they arise, apart from the prying ears that gratuitously offer bad advice. You must work at it together through "thick and thin" until a satisfactory solution is reached. Compromise may be an option, but only if it is not trailed by remorse. When the couple work together to resolve their issues, it engenders good feelings from both and it ratifies that there is a sincere effort being put forth.

The next fundamental principle for maintaining relationships is:

Sacrifice: Requires that you give up your preference so that the other person can have his or hers. This involves the Christian qualities of long suffering and patience. To suffer long is to take the hard times well, trusting that the chords that bind the relationship are strong enough to hold it together through difficult times.

I am the good shepherd: the good
shepherd giveth his life for the sheep.

John 10:11

The attitude portrayed by Jesus is that He is willing to give up His life for His people. We see this also in King David that while he was yet a mere shepherd boy, he faced a lion and then a bear armed only with his sling and his faith in God to bring him the victory in carrying out his duties to protect his sheep. (1Samuel 17:34-37). Jesus' people know they can trust Him, and David's sheep dwelled in the comfort of having a shepherd worthy of trust who would protect them with his own life against attacks from predators. And so it must be between partners in a relationship. Each confident of where the other stands, and confident that they can trust one another to look out for each other's interests and wellbeing, and that they are willing to make necessary sacrifices for one another. It is positive and affirming in the relationship when both are fully committed to sacrificing all that is necessary, the one for the other.

You need not become somber about making sacrifices as you will probably never have to face a situation in which you must sacrifice your life for your partner. There are many other noteworthy sacrifices that can and should be made at least once, and other sacrifices need to be made on an on-going basis. There are opportunities before you daily in which to put into the works a plan for the sacrifice you need to make. To sacrifice is to give up something of value. Most of us have extreme value for our own opinions and, there is something else that you value highly, your pride. You'd rather die than give in when your mind is made up or you are locked into thinking a certain way. Here is where your greatest opportunity to begin to sacrifice for your partner actually lies. Learn to resist fighting for that position you hold so dearly. I'm referring to that sense of, "this is what I believe and I'm sticking to it till death." Rather, give way to your partner's position, or opinion, and sacrifice your ego as you commit to not having to prevail and unilaterally impose your will on your partner.

The next fundamental principle Jesus applied to maintain relationships requires going outside yourself. Going outside yourself is not an easy thing to do. It requires practice and at the beginning, the ability to perform self-assessment, until you are able to gain mastery of it, and it becomes an added skill for bringing balance to the relationship. This next fundamental principle can be summarized as the art of substitution:

Substitution: Put yourself in your partner's place and understand his or her point of view. You have to imagine how to allow the other person in your relationship to express their point of view without voicing your disagreement, imposing your will, needing to provide the solution, being right, or justifying yourself? The underlying issue may be whether you can just listen attentively without interrupting even if you're opposed to what is being said.

> For Christ also hath once suffered
> for sins, the just for the unjust,
> that he might bring us to God,
> being put to death in the flesh, but
> quickened by the Spirit:

1 Peter 3:18

A substitution is taking the place for someone else. I would like to stress substitution in the very narrow sense of you putting yourself in your partner's place at the height of a disagreement. This is ever more crucial in the wake of a disagreement, during a difference of opinion or in the midst of an argument. Stop, pause and consider what your partner is trying to communicate. Put yourself in his or her place and in this instance bear the weight they are holding up, as it pertains to you. Your disagreement is imposing undue weight on your partner. You can temporarily relieve them of the weight they are carrying by letting go of your immediate desire to be heard, to be right, and in your thoughts, substitute their position for yours.

Let us say two friends are discussing politics where one has very liberal views and the other has very conservative views. While having a discussion on a divergent issue, you should not see his conversation as though you were being asked to agree with your friend's point of view. Instead, you should be extending the courtesy of allowing them to express their view. You are being asked to place yourself in the other persons' position momentarily, to make a try at understanding how upsetting it is for the other party (especially a friend) not to have their point of view understood. Not being understood can be mistaken for not allowing them to be heard. Your point of view remains unchanged, but now you can feel how it is when someone is prevented from freely expressing their views. Once you get past the issue of the individual's right to have a divergent opinion, you will come to see that they did not necessarily expect agreement from you either, that they merely wanted you to hear them out and maybe, understand their point of view. In most instances both parties can walk away appeased or even justified in that their point of view was heard and understood, although the parties couldn't convince one another to agree.

When substitution is practiced the relationship is strengthened by mutual trust and respect for each other's point of view. This is of utmost importance in a relationship because it keeps the doors to communication open even when agreement can't be reached.

Another of Jesus fundamental principles is:

Submission: Give in to your partner's point of view. Acknowledge that he or she has a different perspective. Consider it not to be a better or worse idea than yours, simply different. Giving in is not surrendering your valuable convictions.

> And he went a little further, and fell
> on his face, and prayed, saying, O my
> Father, if it be possible, let this cup
> pass from me: nevertheless not as I
> will, but as thou wilt.
>
> *Matthew 26:39*

Occasionally, your partner's point of view is going to make more sense than yours, although you still prefer your own point of view. Sometimes the other perspective won't make as much sense as yours, but it's a viable perspective, just the same. Occasionally you become deeply enmeshed in your own views and think it impossible to let go that opinion and accept someone else's view. When that situation comes up with your partner, if it's not detrimental, this is the time to submit. Let it go. After all, what's the difference between Chinese food and pizza if it's all about eating the food, anyway?

The most divisive moments in a relationship are centered on the inability of one party to submit to the other. When it comes to the order of Christian life, submission is a big problem. Submission should not be a problem to any of us since it is clearly defined in God's Word. "Wives submit to your own husbands", (Ephesians 5 22), which is widely misunderstood, and has become a source for many matrimonial disputes. We find little disagreement in that children are to submit to their parents and that pets are to submit to the kids. However, we can so easily overlook (Ephesians 5:21) which calls us to "submit to one another in the fear of God". We quickly accept that we are to submit to God and that we are to submit to every ordinance of man (the laws of the land), but we encounter resistance and have the most difficult time accepting the concept of submitting to each other. The base line for submitting is to do it out of love, that it's being done for love's sake and in the fear of God. Submission is a principle commonly found in the Scriptures. We are to submit to our elders in the Word, and we are instructed to submit to earthly authorities and spiritual authorities. Without submission you cannot partner with the Lord. You most certainly want to have a wonderful experience every moment in your relationship, and this is a small price to pay, which will bring you many happy returns.

The fifth and last fundamental principle I observed of how Jesus maintained relationships was:

Survival: Persevere in the relationship through difficult times. The survival of a good and healthy relationship is vital, and a higher objective than persevering for yourself.

We are inclined to think of a relationship as a situation pertaining to two people, and that is certainly not an incorrect way to regard a relationship. Let's consider an added view of what constitutes a relationship, and in the process step up that perception to a higher plane. Think about a corporation, it can have one owner, two or many, but it is an entity with an existence of its own, and with perpetuity. A relationship is comprised of two people or more who have agreed to band together to achieve a purpose which they have in common, and who have ownership in that relationship.

But the relationship is also an entity on to itself. You or your partner can and do exist individually outside of the relationship, as you go about conducting your other business and personal affairs. You also engage in other, unrelated relationships. Each relationship is an independent entity from the others. However, the relationship would not exist without you. You each provide the components that comprise the totality of the relationship. You bring the elements that make that relationship work, therefore, the higher the quality of your contribution, the better the quality of the relationship. By putting your best to efforts into the relationship, you enhance the viability of the entity (the relationship) itself, and further insure its survival. You have created a living entity (the relationship) which must be nurtured and supplied with its life's essentials in order for it to thrive. Survival of the relationship requires an on-going contribution on your part, and the more you contribute the more imminent its preservation and success.

> And there arose a great storm of wind,
> and the waves beat into the ship, so
> that it was now full. And he was in
> the hinder part of the ship, asleep on
> a pillow: and they awake him, and say
> unto him, Master, carest thou not that
> we perish? And he arose, and rebuked
> the wind, and said unto the sea, Peace,
> be still. And the wind ceased, and there
> was a great calm.
>
> *Mark 4:37-39*

Fearing for their lives as the boat took in much water and began to sink, the disciples woke Jesus and accused Him of not caring that they were about to perish. Throughout the ordeal, Jesus was comfortably asleep in the back of the boat. Human nature compels us to want others to suffer equally, have to endure the same perils, or worse than us in a crisis. Imagine the men's anguish as they realized they were about to sink and Jesus, the only one able to save them from their impending demise was asleep in the back of the boat.

I cannot imagine that they woke Him calmly with a gentle nudge or soft voices. These men were panic stricken, and they roused Jesus up with the same intensity of their anguish. If this were you or me being wakened in that manner, I am sure that the immediate response to the rude awakening would not be laced with kindness. You know how to cherish that peaceful rest after a hard day's work, and when you find that sweet spot where you are in deep sleep, you yell at the kids if they dare make too much noise and wake you up. Jesus worked very hard all day healing all sorts of sicknesses and disease, giving sight to the blind, and having virtue pass from Him to bless others. I think He cherished His rest. If it were you in His situation, you'd be fierce. But Jesus arose and instantly assessed the situation. He rebuked the wind and calmed the sea, and there was a great calm. Survival from the Lord's point of view was not to rail at the men for their discomposure and to yell back at them. Instead, He took positive and definitive action that calmed the entire situation and even calmed the men. Jesus did not try to make Himself righteous with the men. His soothing actions caused a higher objective to be achieved in that situation, it enhanced the survival of His relationship with the men on the ship.

The concept of survival is key to a successful relationship. It helps you see why you must put personal feelings aside and be a soothing contributor to the solution. All five components are of grave importance to maintaining the relationship in good stead. Should one element be withheld it would cause an imbalance in the relationship, the source of which would be difficult to pinpoint, and it would lead to a default to finding or laying blame on other faults. This is the invisible relations killer. Without the full quiver of the Five Ss' at work, the relationship will experience unexpected quakes that grow into deep fissures that can eventually become insurmountable concerns.

ALWAYS IN REMEMBRANCE (2 PETER 1:15)

1. _____ sets the parties in the relationship apart from everyone else.
2. One should associate with persons who are in _____ of their godly relationship.
3. _____ is giving up your preference for the benefit of others in the relationship.
4. In the process of _____, you place yourself in your partner's position to better understand a divergent point of view.
5. _____ is not surrender, but an acknowledgement of a different perspective.
6. It is vital for a relationship to be healthy for its _____.

SCRIPTURE REFERENCE:

Hebrews 13:12; John 10:11; 1 Peter 3:18; Matthew 26:39; Mark 4:37-39; Ephesians 5:21-22; 1 Samuel 17:34-37; Luke 10:17-18; John 9:27

IV.

Working *to* Build Up *the* Relationship

HIGHER GROUND PRINCIPLE # 5

Apply biblical principles in your relationship.

Know and apply spiritual laws.

It will be difficult to operate and apply what you don't know, so my desire is to lead you in an area of biblical study that needs to be elevated to the top of your priorities. If your desire is to grow in a skill or subject, it is incumbent upon you to learn as much as possible about it before you try putting it into practice. Spiritual laws may at first seem distant and remote from your daily activities and your sphere of knowledge, but as you study spiritual laws you will come to find they are not as remote or foreign as you might think. Spiritual laws are at work in every aspect of your life. They are written and taught throughout the Bible as principles of faith, such that when applied consistently produce the same intended result.

Love, respect, and submission are acts of the will. An act of the will means that you control when and how you exercise it by your own willingness to do it. These three are also prime examples of spiritual principles that yield spiritual fruit, more commonly known as having a godly effect on others. Love, respect, and submission are spiritual principles that when put into effect operate the spiritual law of reciprocity.

"Therefore, all things whatsoever ye would that men should do to you, do ye even so to them: for this is the law and the prophets". (Matthew 7:12) By doing to others as you would have them do unto you, a virtuous cycle is started that will soon yield the most positive interpersonal results. There are many more principles written throughout the Bible and you may want to build your own list to put into practice and to draw upon in your time of need. I encourage you to search the scriptures and add other favorite spiritual principles and personalize your own list. (As a hint I suggest you may want to start with Galatians 5:22—23, the fruit of the spirit.)

Pray for us: for we trust we have a
good conscience, in all things willing
to live honestly.

Hebrews 13:18

You can choose to love, respect, and submit to your partner for the common good of the relationship, and when you do so, you must do it unconditionally, not expecting a reward and without holding a grudge. This describes a spiritual law in application for living life in "good conscience" and honestly in your relationship.

You can also choose to honor the role or authority of the other person in the relationship rather than to be totally opposed to it or find yourself contesting it from time to time. This presumes that you are both clear on the roles to be fulfilled, and the extent to which each of you is charged with and committed to your respective role and responsibilities. If roles and responsibilities are vague, unclear, or not agreed upon, they become a source for resentment and bitterness down the line. Likewise, authority and leadership must also be clear and distinct, and agreed upon if the relationship is to prosper by them and to minimize conflict and hopefully eliminated it.

Are you or your partner taking cues for handling your relationship from sources like TV sitcoms, reality programs or other media productions? Sitcoms and reality programs are the most damaging examples of standards to apply in your relationship. They are created to excite and titillate the audience and to shock their reality. For example, you do not want to find your romantic partner in the manner presented in the "Bachelor" program on tv. The cues for the standards in your relationship should come only from God's Word, because that's the only source of absolute truth, and God's desire is for you to prosper and be in health; which refers to your mental health, as well as the physical. So many relationships are entered into out of ignorance, and they are ruled by the popular theme of the day. Celebrities are mistakenly set as a standard for a relationship without taking into account the poor role models that they generally are when it comes to living in real life. Besides, you don't have the money to live the loose lifestyles that they do, and it takes longer for things to catch up with them than they will with you because they have escape options not likely available to you. They can visit with friends for extended periods of time, go on vacation or take a sabbatical with little or no impact on their financial lives or responsibilities. That, you may not be privy to do. Besides, very few sitcoms last longer than a few seasons as viewers become bored, or the story line ends up at a point it is insupportable. God's Word does not alter to suit the times, and it lives and abides unchanged forever (1 Peter 1:23).

Are you perceived the way you intend to be perceived in the relationship? Only you can choose the manner in which you will comport yourself in each and every relationship. A young woman may choose to act girlish with her boyfriend to appeal to him, perhaps because of her insecurity around him, or perceived competition for his attention from other women. Her lack of assurance leads her to determine that this is the best behavior to getting and retaining his undivided attention. By choosing that type of behavior the young woman is casting herself into a role inviting a corresponding behavior from her boy-friend that she may later find condescending or outright insulting, and if not noticeable at the early stages of the relationship, it is almost certain to become an issue later on. Choose wisely how you present yourself in a relationship so that you elicit the treatment and response commensurate with your expectations and in line with how you desire to be treated. Set the expectations for the relationship on the right track from the onset.

Are you receiving the level of respect that you envisioned for your participation in the relationship? It may be that part of the problem you are having is connected to not being taken as serious as you think you should be, due to the way you are coming across. If you are a prankster and always joking around, you should not expect others to take you seriously. They will marginalize you when it comes to serious issues, because you failed to take things serious in the past. In a relationship, this is a most notable concern in dire need of being worked out. First work on changing to how you want to be perceived, then work on how you perform in front of others. Your partner and associates will only be convinced of a change in you, through consistency and reliability displayed by you over time.

> Then Pharaoh sent and called Joseph,
> and they brought him hastily out of
> the dungeon: and he shaved himself,
> and changed his raiment, and came in
> unto Pharaoh.

Genesis 41: 14

Joseph's desire was to make the right first impression with Pharaoh, an impression that would establish deep trust and confidence in him by Pharaoh. This should be the model for how you present yourself in your relationships, always at your best, and especially when others are forming first impressions about you.

You may have noticed unacceptable patterns of behavior in in your present relationship, or negativity which did not exist before. These less than desirable patterns may suddenly become noticeable, or they can arise subtly, as attitudes and treatment of each other changes. When this occurs, it is a symptom of a malignant behavior pattern that will eat away at the relationship like a cancer. The shortest route for recovery often comes from a renewed appreciation for the other, and behavioral change that puts into practice a loving, courteous and kind treatment where it did not exist before. Among fellow believers a love filled scripture shared together can be the catalyst to center a conversation that leads to a healthy cure, especially between a husband and wife. Great examples of practicable scriptures for situations like this are found in: (Ephesians 5:25 - for husbands acting unlovingly towards their wives; Galatians 5:13 - "by love serve one another", in the case of one or the other acting selfishly). Scripture must not be used to beat someone down or to shame them. At the onset of the conversation scripture can used to set the standard of how God's Word instructs, and your willingness to accept its principles and commandments. If your partner refuses to accept the scripture, pray for them fervently and seek help.

Are you pleased with your role in the relationship? Are you satisfied with what is being expected of you, or do you feel there is an imbalance associated with what is being expected of you? Exploring this will require you to re-visit the origin of the relationship. How did it start, what was the purpose you had in common for forming the relationship, and how has it changed, and what adjustments need to be made? These are extremely relevant questions that may not have easy answers, but which need to be explored with frequency to ensure the relationship is being steered in the desired direction, and not left unattended and derail. In the event things are going astray it is of utmost importance to talk about a change in purpose, and adjust the headings toward the new goal. Start by identifying the near term and achievable revised goals important to the relationship. Then, agree to work together to achieve the new goals and redistribute responsibility and roles, and reassign tasks accordingly. You may discover that once you both are on board with the first set of tasks it will become easier to tackle the next. This new outlook will generate positive energy and wonderful new ideas will flow from the two of you together to cause the relationship to flourish again with renewed vitality. Issues to consider in the framing of your new horizons are:

> What are the relevant positions held or appointed in the relationship and who is to bear responsibility?

> How can we hold each other accountable without causing dissention or disappointment?

> Who will take the lead or fill the role of being the head? (Is the role for a head person needed, does he or she have the acknowledgment and support of the other?

What are the necessary functions and responsibilities in the relationship, and how should they be distributed?

What aspects are unnecessary, what is superfluous, and undesirable in the relationship? (i.e.; What do you not want your relationship to look like or to be like?)

ALWAYS IN REMEMBRANCE (2 PETER 1:15)

1. *To* _____ up my relationship, I should know and apply spiritual laws.
2. Love, respect, and submission are examples of acts of the _____.
3. You should unconditionally love, submit, and respect the other for the _____ good of the relationship.
4. You can choose to _____ the role and authority of others.
5. Leadership and authority must be clear and distinct to avoid _____.
6. Sitcoms and other popular sources are _____ examples of social standards.
7. Do you command or do you demand _____ your relationship?
8. The _____ first impression establishes trust and confidence in your relationship.

SCRIPTURE REFERENCE:

Galatians 5:22—23; Hebrews 13:18; 1 Peter 1:23; Genesis 41: 14

V.

Examining Faults *in the* Relationship

HIGHER GROUND PRINCIPLE # 6

Minimize the potential for failure in your relationship.

We don't want to dwell on failure for too long, but we must take a short side trip to help us determine the factors needed to incur change or that need radical surgery performed to remove dysfunctional aspects in the relationship and prepare it to receive improvement, or to be built up again. Rebuilding the relationship is similar to repairing it, but it involves a more serious overhaul.

Has the relationship entered a vicious cycle? When you prefer to be somewhere else other than at a pre-appointed time and place with your partner, it's a strong sign that something is not going right for you. If such be the case, then your partner is either ahead of you on the curve or shortly behind. You will both soon acknowledge that the relationship is headed for trouble.

A key symptom that tells if your relationship is on the ropes is that every day you allow yourself to say ever increasing and harsher things to your partner, or vise-versa, that lead to arguing or other disappointments. You become increasingly callous toward one another and the attitude becomes less caring every day.

When does the relationship become not worth saving? If there's willingness, the relationship is always worth making every effort to save. You've heard it said that "the grass is greener on the other side" or that "there are plenty of fish in the sea". I will not debate the veracity of either of those colloquialisms, but I will make the case that relationships may have multiple complications and may affect innocent persons through collateral damage when they go sour. One of the first impulses when a partner feels seriously aggrieved is to look outside the relation for comfort and support. In marriage, it starts with friends of the same gender and swiftly migrates to getting attention from the opposite sex. Friends may not be much help either since their counsel too often is to look for someone else to replace the current partner; plenty of fish in the sea.

If your desire to present yourself pure before the Lord, you cannot have weighty baggage holding you down. It is your responsibility to resolve issues that bind you or in any other way prevent or obstruct your relationship with the Lord. If your personal relationship is on the mend, chances are that your relationship with Jesus is not far behind. You are the common denominator in both instances. As things go for you in your earthly life, so will they also go in your spiritual life. You should desire to give your utmost to make your earthly relationships work in godly ways so that you may enjoy a godly relationship with Jesus free of earthly obstructions.

Has the relationship gotten to the point of no return? Is the behavior of either one reprobate and irreparable? This might be a fact if you find yourself acting as though you strongly dislike the other partner and there is no willingness or desire to compromise or change. See (Titus 1:15—16).

Has the relationship become the venue for dishonoring each other between you and your partner at social and family gatherings? A relationship can become so weighty that it incurs derisory behavior on your part. Your hurt feelings, or sensing you are being marginalized will illicit scornful behavior which goes unnoticed by you. Emotions are deluded into taking action that will justify how you feel, which does not go unnoticed by others around you, and especially by your partner. Your family and friends who know you best may be disappointed in the changes they are seeing in your behavior. You can be sure that your behavior did not escape your partner's attention. It's become an escalating upward spiral of negativity at the point of no return.

Do you feel that you are the butt of your partner's bad jokes, that you are often caused to bear insults or made to feel inferior at social gatherings, and that communication is mostly one-way and often condescending? An imbalance in the relationship can cause one or the other partner to become the fall guy, the butt end of someone's jokes and condescending treatment.

A relationship can have the character of an intellectual or an emotional relationship. Emotional relationships are comprised of outbursts and outrageous behavior. This characteristic is depicted in a movie scene where the wife is destructively hurling dishes at her husband in a fit of anger. Although generally short-lived, these outbursts can be the source of escalation leading to abusive language or even physical violence. The effect of emotional outbursts may not be anticipated beforehand, but they can be very costly in both dollars and emotional capital of the relationship. Forgiveness on the part of the parties is hard to come by after such a display of behavior, and the event is definitely going to leave a hard to heal scar regarding trusting the partner in future similar situations of erratic or unprovoked displays. Prepare yourself mentally to avoid blow outs, and if you encounter difficulty in achieving this, consider that a medical exam could be prudent to identify hormonal or chemical imbalances that need treatment by a qualified physician. Women undergoing menopause should have their behavior in check, and you should each take care to minimize confrontations when one or both are stressed. So called "make-up sex" might be a good experience, but is not a reliable source for permanently making up and correcting the deficiency in the relationship.

Intellectual relationships, in contrast are guarded, perhaps they become too guarded. In this type of relationship communication is kept to a minimum and only for essential purposes. Little is communicated with honesty. This characteristic is mostly ruled by silence or unrelated topics dominating the conversations between you. These conversations are polite and managed to avoid or skirt around the issues at hand. You may prefer to dwell at this level because it provides a barrier of protection from your emotions running amok, and for maintain a comfortable place where you are sheltered from dealing with the harsh topics and other unsavory things. Men are more likely to employ this tactic defensively for fear of being drawn into a fight with words they are ill prepared to engage in, and a fight they are certain to lose. Men are very competitive and do not like to lose. The truth behind the tactic in this case becomes evident and both parties by silent agreement consent not to deal with the issue at hand, at least for the time being. The after effects of avoiding the topic are long lasting and forgiveness rarely comes in time to bail out the relationship. These are the elements that make up the hidden reasons why in a marriage one spouse wants a divorce and the other is ambivalent as to why. Intellectual relationships should be avoided from ruling your life, and you should start taking measures to deal with this tactic right away. The longer you wait to handle the matter, the more complicated and vague the facts become.

Are you both operating on the same plane and with the same set of facts? It is possible that you are each approaching the problem from divergent views and your opinions are not even in the same ball park. You can recognize this when the two of you cannot sit together for a moment before contention sets-in, in one form or another, but always prompted by the sensitivity of an unresolved issue left untouched by either of you. There is a remedy for starting to deal with treatment for this, it is called listening. The most important thing about listening is that you are not talking when you are listening, and in this case, you are going to listen for a long time. It is important though, that you acknowledge what is being said, and that you elect not to respond to it, at least not at this time. Be sure to agree on a time in the future for you to respond to the concerns raised by your partner that reflect on the two of you, and that you both are aware of a clear intent to respond.

The elements of communication 101 are: listen, consider, and then speak words to edify. Respond with a soft answer, gentleness, and kindness. See (Proverbs 15:1, 17—18).

How much are you taking from the relationship without putting back? In some relationships the imbalance takes the form of one person being the giver and the other, well simply put, is the taker. What's odd about this is no one likes being taken for granted, or better yet taken advantage of to the end of feeling abused. It is up to you to guard against such abusive behavior by others upon you. But entering into a relationship should be an honest decision for the betterment of both, or to achieve a common purpose where the results are equitable to the level of effort each partner puts into it. All that said, there exist individuals who seek opportunities where they can profit in some way with minimum contribution, and there are others who are willing subjects, accepting to contribute substantially more than their equitable portion, for the sake of having a relationship with a particular person. Neither of these conditions present an optimal case for a good relationship, and the relationship will eventually fold. Relationships are like bank accounts in the sense that the partners take withdrawals from it. However, if there is no replenishment the relationship will become bankrupt.

> Let him that stole steal no more, rather
> let him labor that he may have to give to
> him that needeth.

Ephesians 4:28

It is up to you to stop taking more than you are entitled to from the relationship, and to start making a sufficient contribution back into the relationship, to carry your own weight. If your partner is the one in need, then work to provide your partner with the rudimentary help to build him or her up so you can both prosper and be contributors in the relationship.

Have you become more apart from each other than a part of each other? When you are together it might seem best for you to just sit there and silently enjoy the tv program, or you may prefer to roll out a book and immerse vicariously into another realm than to make conversation or exchange tales with your partner about your day's activities. You have diminished your quality time together in exchange for a purgatorial existence. You may prefer to put distance between each other, taking on other obligations or volunteering for things that consume your time, or you are hiding behind the excuse of waning circumstances letting ambivalence rule the relationship. It may seem as a new discovery to you, but this is the formula to render relationships null and void, and it has been the tool over the ages for lazy and unwilling partners to let the relationship find its own course.

If there is willingness, you can work change into your circumstances. You will have to give up something in order to spend more time in the relationship, or it may require the sacrifice of something of great value to repair and save the relationship. You must commit in full to apply yourself to rebuilding your relationship, and the first step is to get your partner on board with you, and together in marching step.

ALWAYS IN REMEMBRANCE (2 PETER 1:15)

1. Ever increasing harsh treatment is a symptom of _____ in the relationship.
2. Can you identify if your relationship has entered into a _____ cycle?
3. A relationship is reprobate when one or more persons are _____ to compromise.
4. Basic elements to communication include _____ considering what is said, and speaking words to edify.
5. A soft answer, gentleness, and kindness help to _____ tension in a relationship.
6. An _____ relationship is comprised of outbursts and outrageous behavior.
7. An intellectual relationship is too _____; little is communicated with THIS.
8. Your partner may be in need of being _____ in the relationship.
9. Closeness and time spent _____ helps to build up the relationship.
10. To succeed, you may be called upon to make _____ in your relationship.

SCRIPTURE REFERENCE:

Titus 1: 15—16; Proverbs 15: 1, 17—18; Ephesians 4:28

VI.

Building Success Into
the Relationship

HIGHER GROUND PRINCIPLE # 7

Build a virtuous cycle in your relationship
through hard work.

In order to successfully build up a relationship, you must take the initiative to start a virtuous cycle. Virtuosity does not come easily to a decaying relationship. It requires hard work, sacrifice, investing in all-out effort to make repairs, and setting aside your pride. Whole heartedly take on the new role and become the change agent for the better.

You can begin to effect change by being the first to do something positive. Build patterns of successes into your routines that encourage one another and that inspire kindness, gentleness, and favorable treatment from each other. Review the fundamentals of the Five Ss' and be sure that you are applying them. This is a good time and place to start applying them aggressively. In the marriage, a little flirtation can go a long way to reciprocity with kindness and pleasantness.

Compliment, don't criticize:

We are each gifted with an innate ability to point out others' weaknesses and short comings. We are never short of answers or suggestions to correct someone else's faults no matter how insensitive or callous our suggestions might be. I have seen brutal criticism taken to unimaginable heights in retaliation against the person you cherish so dearly. It is healthier to find some way to compliment your partner than to criticize him or her. It is painstakingly difficult to compliment someone when you are reeling from emotional hurt they have caused you. But, repairing a broken relationship is achievable and essential. You can adopt a system of behavior that enables you to be the kindest to others when you are suffering the most pain. Being kind to your partner when he has gouged the goodness out of you is what makes you Christ like. Remember that on the cross He said, "Father for give them" because they did not know what they were doing. People get caught up in their own causes and become blinded by that unintentionally injure their loved ones, they know not what they do. And you display mercy through a virtuous role that is forgiving.

And not only so, but we glory in
tribulations also: knowing that
tribulation worketh patience; And
patience, experience; and experience,
hope: And hope maketh not ashamed;
because the love of God is shed abroad
in our hearts by the Holy Ghost which
is given unto us.

Romans 5:3—5

Build consistency in your relationship:

The most difficult thing you can be asked to do is to contradict your convictions, and bring on a change of mind. The hardest undertaking you will undergo in your relationship is to change your own mind while entangled in a controversy. Your opinion is set in stone based on the experiences you've had in life that affirm your opinion is correct. There is no room in your head for any thought contrary to the outcome you desire. In this kind of situation, you need to change your mind from its present conviction into believing something different that will improve relations. Your current stance on what you believe is right, is leading to the opposite of what would be in the best interest of the relationship. Sometimes it's your life's experiences that push you to do the contrary of what you should do when it comes to repairing the relationship. Instead of giving in and embracing a new path, your pride pushes you in the opposite direction. Your desire to kiss and make-up is trumped by your way of thinking, and you can't bring yourself to doing the right thing. You'd rather remain angry and apart, than to give in. You must bring change to your mind, a change which encourages a new and different way of perceiving things at a higher level of thinking than you are accustomed to. You must convince your mind to allow you to take that first step for moving forward in a positive direction. Then, you can continue to take bigger and more frequent steps until you are running at full speed with your heart and mind in the direction of your loved one. You must work to master putting pride and other inhibitors behind you. And then you can aspire to obtain peace with your partner and seek ways to be a blessing and to not allow yourself to be drawn away by negative thoughts. Don't recompense evil with evil, but rather, be the one with the renewed mind reminding yourself that this person is a very valuable part of your life, and that you don't want that to change. (Romans 2:14-18).

Some valuable points to help the reconciliation:

How big an effort are you willing to make to get your relationship to work well, and how much risk are you willing to take to obtain the right results? We take risks going into business, changing jobs, relocating, and even driving to the grocery store. Why then are you so guarded with your emotions when it comes to your relationship? The answer lies in the degree to which you value other things compared to your relationship. As you release your emotional attachment to other things, you become less guarded about the things you value outside the relationship, and place the focus on helping your relationship to grow.

You need to learn and put into practice ways to nourish the relationship. In marriage, as well as in other relationships, it can begin with more intimacy and in sharing daily life experiences, exercising THIS one hundred percent of the time, setting time aside to spend together, participating in each other's preferred activities, and alternating the things that are special to either one. Other ideas include dating and giving each other special little gifts. (Everyone likes pleasant surprises; be original with yours.)

Are you experiencing a crisis in leadership, and need validation for keeping the relationship on track?

Two cannot make a democracy. One has to lead and make essential decisions, and the other should be willing to concede and in good conscience submit in agreement. Compromise is not the best solution in a relationship. A compromise between two persons may yield undesirable results with lasting consequences and the harboring of ill feelings. Submission, although strange to our ears, is the call of the Christian in a godly relationship to concede. By making a conscious decision to concede, you are making a commitment to fully support the decision you have accepted. Making a concession can quell anxieties and bring instant peace. (1 Corinthians 11:3 and Ephesians 5:23).

How are decisions made in your relationship?

What method do you employ for identifying problems and root their causes in your relationship? What is your plan for dealing with issues and finding a way to correct them? Your response may be a shrug, or if you want to honestly resolve them, you might start by saying, "I don't know".

Finding the right path will not be brutally painful, or extremely embarrassing, when your choice is borne out of love. 1 Peter 4:8 reminds us that love shall cover a multitude of sins. The human mind has a propensity to stay focused on the negative and you must work hard to change that focus so that you can see the brighter lining in the dark clouds that hover over your relationship. I have experienced the effect of negativity when elated with good news, but others would not share in my joy. On occasion, I have delivered what I thought was great news only to have my joy dampened by a negative acknowledgement. You're familiar with instances like these. The participants are like "prophets of doom" gushing out negative comments that you don't expect to receive from family and friends. You say to your spouse, "Honey, we just paid off the Visa card," and her response is "Well, what are you going to do about the Master card?" It's sort of depressing, isn't it? I have caught myself similarly spewing sarcasm where it wasn't warranted as a retaliation for when it was done to me, or just to be cool with the rest of the crowd. I hope I have been forgiven, as I hope you too will forgive when it happens to you. I've repented from having done this, and I promise never again to do it to anyone else. Instead of rejoicing at the good news, we cast gloom and cause rejection where it's the least warranted, in the relationship. It is a human tendency to cause rejection and to lay guilt on others when we should be the authors of sharing in joy with the people in our lives.

If you pause to think about how much you love and admire the person you are with, perhaps your reaction would be one of support and encouragement. To begin the relational upward spiral, you must commit to inviting the Lord into your relationship and having Him establish permanent residence with you, there. Identify the problem that needs attention, and commit with your partner to pray for it together on a daily basis until it is completely gone. Organize your thinking and plan to pray without bringing up your opinion on what caused the problem (his laziness, her shopping, etc.), but pray only that the Lord will tenderize both your hearts and open your understanding so that you may receive His guidance, His methods, and how to apply them. Your relationship is going to blossom and show improvement quickly.

Bringing more value to the relationship for its prosperity

This issue should not be taken lightly. You need to ask yourself, "What proactive measures can I take to become more encouraging to my partner?" This is an important fundamental for leading the partners to promote caring and openness about decisions affecting the relationship that are yet to be made, or that need re-thinking. One way to add value to the relationship is by not allowing your daily life to become so routine that one or both of you loses heart, or by letting the relationship become perfunctory, without meaning. Should you find yourself doing or saying vain, hollow and empty things with little purpose or no intent of acting on them in a joint plan of action with accountability, take note that your relationship is in or about to be in crisis. You will want to discuss this concern and make plans with real timetables, budgets, and distribution of assignments, as well as responsibility, and above all with real intent to fulfill them. This is it. This is how decisions get made in your relationship to keep it vibrant and prosperous, with the full participation of all participants.

ALWAYS IN REMEMBRANCE (2 PETER 1:15)

1. By taking the initiative, you can start a _____ cycle.
2. Doing _____ things builds patterns of success.
3. The hardest work takes place in the _____.
4. Letting go of your _____ depends on how big of a risk you are willing to take.
5. Pleasant surprises _____ the relationship.
6. How _____ are made affect the overall health of the relationship.
7. How do you plan to resolve issues and _____ the relationship?
8. Nourishing the needs of your partner adds _____ and builds up the relationship.

SCRIPTURE REFERENCE:

Romans 5:3—5; Romans 12: 14—21; 1 Corinthians 11:3; Ephesians 5:22; 1 Peter4:8

VII.

APPLYING WORD KNOWLEDGE

HIGHER GROUND PRINCIPLE # 8

Assert your right to leadership through sacrifice and service.

D o you Lord it over others in the relationship?

And why call ye me, Lord, Lord, and do not the things which I say?

Luke 6:46

In Christ's teachings, we have the basic rudiments prescribed for a healthy relationship. You are denying Him when you choose to do the contrary of what He commands. If you are not obeying Him, then He is not your Lord.

Be worthy to call Him Lord.

It is inherent in human nature to prefer having others to wait on you. That is why the travel and leisure industry does so well. People enjoy having someone to serve them, pick up after them, and feed them on time. Aside from pandering alcoholic beverages to travelers, being waited on and served is the trademark of cruise ships. These services and the form of treatment you get on a ship are the benefit you pay for in order to leisurely enjoy your vacation. It is something you pay for. But in a personal relationship being waited on at your leisure is not something one can buy; being spoiled is the byproduct of the happiness of your partner imparting their joy and desire to care for you. To expect to be waited on all the time by your partner, most certainly rubs contrary to any godly way to relate among friends and family. A healthy relationship is reciprocal and not heavily weighted in favor of one or the other. The Christian attitude of service is all about giving and receiving that is not centered on obtaining material gain, or getting undeserved benefits.

> He riseth from supper, and laid aside his garments; and took a towel, and girded himself. After that he poureth water into a bason, and began to wash the disciples' feet, and to wipe them with the towel wherewith he was girded.
>
> *John 13:4—5*

A true leader sets the example. He or she is willing to make sacrifices and offerings for the benefit of others. The leader in the family should constantly be on the lookout for opportunities where he or she can be of service or make provision for other family members before the need arises, and certainly to satisfy a need that could impact negative on the family. Likewise, every leader should be alert to identify opportunities, or to give up his comfort as a sacrifice for someone else. In this fashion, the Word of God comes alive in practice as the one who serves the most is the greatest. Don't let your partner out-serve you.

So after he had washed their feet, and
had taken his garments, and was set
down again, he said unto them, Know
ye what I have done to you? Ye call me
Master and Lord: and ye say well; for so
I am. If I then, your Lord and Master,
have washed your feet; ye also ought to
wash one another's feet. For I have given
you an example, that ye should do as
I have done to you. Verily, verily, I say
unto you, The servant is not greater than
his lord; neither he that is sent greater
than he that sent him. If ye know these
things, happy are ye if ye do them.

John 13: 12—17

If you want joy and happiness in your present life, you must be willing to sacrifice your pride and comfort, and to lay aside the desire to be the sole beneficiary being waited on by your partner, and contribute your share of the labor in the relationship. You have this "god given" opportunity to be the leader in your relationship by demonstrating the Christ-like qualities of giving and serving first, without requiring recompense. Christ demonstrated this Himself by doing the lowliest of tasks for His disciples and did not require of them to do the same for Him. He told His disciples that He had given them an example so that they would do for others as He did for them. They witnessed unfathomable love and unyielding commitment to serve them on His part. Christ is not only your example, He is also your Lord, and you acknowledge that He is your Lord, when you obey His command.

ALWAYS IN REMEMBRANCE (2 PETER 1:15)

1. Exerting pressure on others to get what you want is _____ it over them.
2. You deny Jesus's Lordship when you do differently than He _____.
3. Expecting others to _____ us does not strengthen our relationship.
4. The Christian attitude of service is defined in that one desires to _____.
5. _____your preferences are a quality for Christian living.
6. The _____ example of acceptable leadership is set by Jesus.
7. The _____of the family should be Prepared to be of service to the others.
8. A willingness to sacrifice will bring _____ and happiness to your life.

SCRIPTURE REFERENCE:

Luke 6:46; John 13:4-5; John 13:12-17

PART

VIII.

QUALITIES *for* CHRISTIAN LIVING

HIGHER GROUND PRINCIPLE # 9

Live and walk by the higher and greater standard worthy of the Christian name.

As a Christians, you have a very special charge and responsibility. You accepted Jesus Christ as your Lord to live according to the principles and precepts that He taught and that have been committed to us in God's Word. That responsibility goes beyond just living your life in obedience. It also includes teaching biblical precepts to others. If you desire to have a godly relationship, no one is in greater need of knowing the biblical principles that you know than the other person in your relationship.

However, before you can teach biblical precepts to others, you must acquire the knowledge from the Word for yourself. Then, when you know something worthy of sharing, and after you have put it into practice for yourself, then you can offer it up and lead by the example, as well. Being a Christian is a very high calling. You may have previously heard the term "high calling" used in matters related to the church. It is not only a calling from above, but is also a calling for you to rise higher than where you presently are spiritually, and to rise above others in exercising THIS. If your public or private behavior is the same as everybody else's, if you are reacting adversely to someone because you think it's cool or because that's the way people around you are behaving, believing it's the cool and acceptable thing to do, or if you tell someone off because it's the popular thing to do among the company you are keeping, then you are no better than others in the world. In fact, your life is centered in the world's ways and your conversation is not in Christ, but in the world (Romans 1:32). Why would anyone seeing the type of behavior you're displaying view you any different than they see themselves, and despise you for the same reasons they despise their tormentors. They could not imagine following you into the Kingdom of God (2 Thessalonians 3:7). Jesus asked you to follow in His steps so that when others follow in your steps they are actually walking in the steps of Jesus Christ. If your hang-out buddies won't consider living by your godly principles, then you may want to exchange those acquaintances for new ones who will bring blessings and virtue into your life.

You must move beyond the popular ways. Settling for how others conduct themselves as acceptable behavior opens the door for entering into a poor relationship in which you will not find the peace and comfort you long for. You have to get past the world's way of thinking and beyond the lifestyle of the ungodly. Using the same thinking pattern as those around you will lead you into incongruous behavior untypical of a Christian. You need to realize that the Lord has made you better than what the world tempts you to be. You need to rise up alongside the Lord to the higher plane of the higher calling. The concept of partnering up with Jesus in your walk through life is what I want you to draw from God's Word throughout this study on relationships. It is up to you to take the initiative to make every one of your relationships work.

Form relationships with others who can become important components and contributors to your life's work. If you are in a situation where you can't see yourself sharing openly in a relationship with a particular person who is an integral part of your family unit or circle of friends, or who is failing to be a benefit in your life, prepare yourself for the challenge ahead in leading them to gain a desire for a relationship with Christ and reach the higher ground, like you have. First, gird yourself for the long haul by committing to consistent prayer for the Lord's intercession, for guidance and for wisdom. Colossians 2:2-3 says, " that their hearts may be comforted, being knit together in love, and unto all riches of the full assurance of understanding, to the acknowledgement of the mystery of God, and of the Father, and of Christ; in whom are hid all the treasures of wisdom and knowledge." Then, when you are better prepared, you can help to shore up the breaches in the other person's life so that you can both come closer together in the relationship. (Galatians 6:2).

Most of the values that get adopted into a relationship are not the values the Lord taught. In other words, your values when applied to a situation may have been drawn from the old-man you, when you were not walking in the steps of the Lord. This happens when you react spontaneously because subconsciously you are taken back to your old habits, even while you are laboring to adopt new ways. There is a tendency to say, "I'm not going to put up with that", because your old way of thinking esteems you better than the other person, or "Because of my position," or "I'm older, therefore he has to respect me." A while back I had a phone confrontation with one of the officers of the firm I work at. He had violated client confidentiality and I wanted to make him aware of it. It wasn't the first time we'd had this similar encounter. As he became heated about my calling him to question, he asked in a very loud voice, "DO YOU KNOW WHO I AM"? My old ways kicked in and I thought to tell him that if he wasn't sure he should check his drivers license, but virtuosity kicked in just in time, and instead I said, "I sure do, that's why I called you". My response could've been of an even higher calling to further defuse the situation and to allow it to end in a civil tone, but that's the best I could muster up at that time. I hope you can see how important it is to practice peace and patience, since you won't know when you are going to need to apply godly wisdom over earthly reaction when provoked by the behavior of others. What I did was not biblically correct, but I'm glad that I now could see the difference. It is up to you to respect others, even if you are in the right. Retaliation only escalates and prolongs a conflict which could've been contained. The Lord says the one who serves the most will be the greatest. If you want to be great, then you have to serve the needs of others regardless of their station in life, and you must prefer others before yourself. Humility and meekness should be the order of the day at all times for you. You must get started on fulfilling this quest today, right now, to find your peaceful place in the Lord. (Galatians 5:13).

As a Christian, you should always bear in mind the qualities that permit you to live in the world peaceably with as little friction as possible in your relationships with others. This can be studied from two separate points of view. One view concerns yourself, and it is required that you not offend or cause abrasion to others (Philippians 1:10). We want to study that separately from the second view, which is what happens when someone offends you. What do you do then? I'm assuming you are not sure what the best course of action to take is, so I will share the Word's principles on this with you.

First, you need to adopt a code of conduct for handling offenses and abrasions, both when you are the cause and when others precipitate the cause. When others offend you, you have to have the right code of conduct deeply inculcated in your heart, so that you can draw upon the proper biblical resources that will enable you to handle your response in a correct and diffusing manner. Correctly means according to principles from the Word. An incorrect response is popular in the eyes of others, but you will steer clear of those when you are living in a renewed mind state. You have to be aware of trying to guard your reputation, especially when there are by standers witnessing the incident, ready to judge you if the behavior is unbecoming. You may feel good at the expense of the other person and if the behavior is contrary or inconsistent with the Word, you will soon feel the weight of your evil ways. Be prepared for the challenges you'll face by:

Having a personal code of conduct is to not offend or cause abrasion with others.

Adopt a code of conduct for handling in coming offenses and abrasions caused by others.

ALWAYS IN REMEMBRANCE (2 PETER 1:15)

1. Christians have a very special charge and _____.
2. _____ Jesus Christ as Lord in your life commits you to obeying Him.
3. Christians should know and _____ biblical principles to others.
4. Being a Christian is a very high _____.
5. Your _____ should not be the same as others.
6. You must apply the _____ taught by the Lord in your relationship.
7. You should have a _____ of conduct to apply in adverse situations.
8. Your personal code of conduct is to not _____ others.

SCRIPTURE REFERENCE:

Romans1:32; 2 Thessalonians 3:7; Galatians 6:2; Galatians 5:13; 1 Corinthians 13: 11—12

IX.

OFFENSES COMMITTED
by YOU

Your commitment as a card-carrying Christian is to be the peacemaker, the light bearer, and the salt of the earth to flavor life all around you with goodness, kindness, compassion and being the example of what a life in Jesus should represent. Before stepping out to put these callings to work, you must ponder the corresponding precepts and fully embrace them with a commitment to carrying them out to their fullest extent. These precepts are the means by which unnecessary social pressure on you and on those in your proximity is minimized; the unnecessary pressures that are caused by offenses inflicted upon you and offenses you inflict on others which have a lasting effect.

And the seed whose fruit is
righteousness is sown in peace by those
who make peace.

James 3:18

The Peacemaker

HIGHER GROUND PRINCIPLE # 10

Be a peacemaker who brings calm to every relationship.

Scripture Reference:

> Deceit is in the heart of them that
> imagine evil: but to the counsellor of
> peace is joy.

Proverbs 12:20

Those who make peace do not accomplish it solely by their good deeds. We know from the history of wars that men have not embraced enduring peace. When peace is brought on in a godly way, it is the product of a seed from the fruit of righteousness. That is to say, that the means employed in the ensuing peace were means eongruent with God's way and were right with God. A peacemaker, we may conclude, is a believer who is walking with God step for step in the footsteps of Jesus.

In the section of scripture we refer to as the Beatitudes, the Lord proclaims that peacemakers are blessed and that they shall be called the children of God (Matthew 5:9). This sets for us the light in which God has framed the value of a peacemaker. As the peacemaker, you become invaluable to the perseverance of the Church, and you become the preserver of peace in your relationships. If you desire to have a healthy relationship, you will need to cover it with peace and use peace as the safety net when things in your relationship start to slip. Only you can operate peace in your life, and you alone are equipped by the Holy Spirit to bring and maintain peace in every relationship.

A peacemaker is best characterized as one who brings calm to a tumultuous situation. We saw previously a wonderful example of how this calm is manifested in Matthew 8:23—27 where the Lord enters a boat with the disciples, and is asleep while they battle a storm. The boat is about to sink and the disciples are in a panic. They fear the boat will sink and that they will drown. Having been in a severe storm in a small boat with my wife and two adolescent children, I sympathize with the disciples knowing firsthand the degree of fear the forces of nature can instill in the heart. One loses hope rather quickly, and a dreadful fear for life sets in fast when the elements of nature get out of control and your only hope is that the storm passes quickly. We prayed and put on life jackets, and in a few minutes that seemed like an eternity, the storm lifted and the Long Island Sound became calm enough to navigate back to the dock. My kids will never forget that horrific, though short lived, experience.

The disciples ultimately run to the back of the boat to wake up and beckon Jesus to intercede. They said, "Save us Lord. We are perishing!" I'm reasonably sure that there were big exclamation points at the end of that sentence, and that they were most likely screaming it out. The Lord, in a calm voice asks, "Why are you afraid?" Then He rebuked the winds and the sea, and it became perfectly calm. His effect on the others was to bring calm and, as peacemaker, to bring enduring peace. This is what you are called upon to do in critical situations where others are in a panic. Your responsibility is to exercise your peace to bring calm to the situation, and it is never more critical than during episodes begging for you to bring peace into the relationship. And although your old nature is yearning to scream back or to yell out a few obscenities, being the peacemaker to bring calm to the episode is at no other time more critical and important than this time.

As the peacemaker, you are equipped with various attributes that prepare you for the duty of improving relationships. There are other attributes essential to that role, and I encourage you to embrace two other precepts that, when applied, invoke the fullness of God's power over the prevailing circumstances. One of these concepts is to be the salt of the earth, and the other is to be the light of the world.

ALWAYS IN REMEMBRANCE (2 PETER 1:15)

1. Christians are called upon to be _____.
2. Applying biblical precepts will diminish unnecessary _____ in your relationship.
3. _____ peace is appropriated through godly works.
4. Peacemakers are _____.
5. Peacemakers shall be called the _____ of God.
6. As Peacemaker, you become the _____ of peace in your relationship.
7. You are _____ to operate peace in your relationship.
8. A Peacemaker brings _____ into a tumultuous situation.
9. A Peacemaker's _____ on others is to calm them

SCRIPTURE REFERENCE:

James 3:18; Proverbs 12:20; Matthew 5:9; Matthew 8:23-27

THE SALT *of the* EARTH

HIGHER GROUND PRINCIPLE # 11

Keep the salt flavor for God's Word in you from diluting by temptation and sin.

Ye is the salt of the earth: but if the salt
have lost his savour, herewith shall it be
salted?

Lord Jesus's exhortation is that you compare your usefulness to that of salt. If you are the salt of the earth, you are the one who infuses flavor into the earth, at least in a spiritual sense. If you have lost your saltiness, then who is going to flavor you? Where is your flavor going to come from? This is the comparison the Lord is making. You are the salt. You are the one God has called through Jesus. You are the one that has been given the charge. You are the one that has been given the responsibility. If you ignore or refuse to apply these principles in your life, where is your help going to come from? You will be salt less! What good are you then?

... It is thenceforth good for nothing...

When you act like everyone else around you are acting, you are good for nothing, because you have lost your salt. You have lost the high calling for what you were commissioned to do. What good are you then?

... but to be cast out, and to be trodden
underfoot of men...

Matthew 5 13-14

Our joint commitment with the Lord is to be peacemakers, to be light bearers, and to be the salt of the earth that flavors the lives of others around us. When you are at peace, the people around you receive that peace, and they will also become peaceful. When you are vociferous, noisy, and argumentative, that is exactly what you will give off, and everybody around you will be inclined to treat each other, and especially you, the same way. Being ostentatious or disrespectful licenses others to treat you the same way, and makes it an acceptable way to behave. But remember, you are the salt; it is up to you to add the flavor to the conversation and set the tone for acceptable behavior. Therefore, you cannot, for example, expect others to be the peacemakers who calm the situation since they simply don't possess the wherewithal to enable peace and infuse a godly flavor into the conversation. When you add salt to water it dissolves and spreads equally to all parts of the water. It is incumbent upon you to be the initiator and to apply the fundamental precepts of being the salt of the earth. You alone have to do it in every situation you are present in. You alone have the salt in you to flavor the situation.

If you are the salt, then you cannot afford to lose your flavor. If you lose your flavor, what or who is going to flavor you? When salt loses its flavor, it is good for nothing. It can't be used. Salt is not only used for seasoning; it is also used as a preservative in food. Your presence, wherever your travels take you, place you int the position of preserving decorum and godly peace. 1 Corinthians 14:40 says to " Let all things be done decently and in order" In your presence there is to be order and decency because it is you who is charged to flavor the conversation.

"Bacalao" is salted codfish, which can last indefinitely without refrigeration. Likewise, you are preserved by the salt of God's Word. When you are preserved in the salt, you can go anywhere, but especially where the spirit leads you. It makes no difference who you happen to come in contact with. You can maintain your saltiness because it's dissolved throughout your entirety. The salt of the spirit is integrally within you and no one can remove it, except you allow it to wash out. This is a good analogy for describing the Word of God resting within you. As some of it gets washed out in the course of the day, you get to put it back and to add even more of it. When you have the Word of God deep in your heart with conviction—when you are not allowing anyone to come along and rinse it out of your life with a bad word, a bad thought, or with a bad attitude, then, you are fulfilling the high calling. When someone has a bad attitude, you're going to turn to him and say, "Gee, are you having a bad day? Perhaps I can pray for you." Or you might say something very nice to that person that helps them come down a few notches, and they are going to back off, because in Proverbs 15:1 the Bible says, "A gentle answer turns away wrath" (NASB). But if someone is having a hard time, or making a hard time of something, and you step out and give them an equally hard time, then the situation is only going to get worse for everyone. Always bear in mind that you are the salt of the earth, and without its flavor, salt is completely useless.

Salt is good: but if the salt have lost his
saltness, wherewith will ye season it?
Have salt in yourselves, and have peace
one with another.

Mark 9:50

When you live by the precept of being the salt of the earth, you are going to have peace, and you are going to make peace. God's Word exhorts you to have peace and to be the peacemaker with those who are in your proximity.

Salt is good: but if the salt have lost his
savour, wherewith shall it be seasoned?
It is neither fit for the land, nor yet for
the dunghill; but men cast it out. He
that hath ears to hear, let him hear.

Luke 14:34-35

Salt is a mineral composed of chlorine and sodium. When these two elements are combined, they serve a useful purpose. You can use these combined elements to accomplish wonderful things. But when it has lost its flavor, all you have is a block of white powder that is good for nothing. It won't even decompose and needs to be trodden over, ground down into a fine dust in order for it to go away. Flavorless salt is a nuisance. That describes what you become when you are living in the sin of the world instead of walking by the Word of God. You are not going to effect change in anyone's life with a negative attitude or by retorting with a smart saying when what the person needs is a blessing in the form of kindness or compassion. Make sure that your salt flavor doesn't dilute by daily "flavoring-up", that is to "flavor-up" by daily studying the Word, reading it, concentrating on it, memorizing it, and praying for God's help to keep your mind stayed on His Word.

ALWAYS IN REMEMBRANCE (2 PETER 1:15)

1. As Christians, we are committed to be _____
2. We are commanded to be the _____ of the earth.
3. If you are the salt, where does your _____ come from?
4. If salt loses its flavor, it is _____ for nothing.
5. We flavor and preserve others' _____ with God's Word.
6. By being at peace, we _____ of our peace with others around us.

SCRIPTURE REFERENCE:

Matthew 5:13-14; Mark 9:50; Luke 14:34-35

The Light *of the* World

HIGHER GROUND PRINCIPLE # 12

Illuminate darkened hearts, help bear another's
heavy load, and bring cheer to the sad.

> Ye are the light of the world. *[Called*
> *to be a light of the world; this is another*
> *really good thing.]* A city that is set on a
> hill cannot be hid.
>
> *Matthew 5:14*

As a bearer of light, you are committed to bring light into dark situations and dark places. You are the center of hope, goodness, kindness, and godliness. (How many of you would like to join the Light Bearers club?) Light Bearers illuminate darkened hearts, bring cheer into the otherwise lackluster lives of people around them, help to bear the load weighing others down, and remove obstacles that obscure the vision from before their brethren's eyes. If you want, you too can join in this purpose, which is led by Jesus Christ. 1 John 1:5 says, "God is light and in Him is no darkness at all". God is the original source of light, and His presence dispels all darkness. He sent His only Son, the Lord Jesus to be the light of the world, and to impart of His light to all who will accept it, so that darkness will be cast out of their lives and they too can bring light to them who dwell in darkness.

Let your light so shine before men that
they may see your good works, [that
they might see the goodness, that they
might see that you are at the center of
hope, that they can see the Godliness
in you], and glorify your Father which
is in heaven.

Matthew 5:16

The image which I want to impart with you here is that you are a beacon of light in a world of darkness. You are a walking lighthouse and a beacon bringing light into the darkness wherever you go. You can focus with others on the issues causing darkness to dwell in their lives, at the same time you bring light into their otherwise darkened environment, as a lamp lights up a dark room, so will you light up the person's life. You bring light into the dark situations and the dark places around you. You are a beacon of God's light that can only be extinguished by you turning it off or placing a covering over your light. Yes, you can dim your light if you put a cover over yourself and hide that glorious light, but that light should be burning furiously within you. A cover over your lamp would consist of acts of sin on your part, or accepting the sins of others. The light in you should be burning so bright at all times that you either let it out or burst at the seams. You must let out your shining light to permeate forth into the pervasive darkness around you.

If you were standing in a dark room and lit a match, the little bit of light from that match would dispel the darkness. One little ray of light dispels darkness, and you are God's little ray of light in the world. Wherever you are, and however dark the situation may be, you are the light, and it is incumbent upon you to shine your light all around and aim the beacon of light to the specific causes of darkness. Agree with me that from now on you're going to let that light shine, to cause it to burn bright and be noticed by those in darkness. You're going to polish the outside and the inside of the lens to make sure that God's light gets reflected through you into the world.

In 2005, my twelve-year-old daughter Loli, Dolores, and I made the 203-step climb up a narrow spiraling, scary staircase to the top of the tallest lighthouse in Florida, the Ponce De Leon Inlet Lighthouse. The most impressive thing I learned that day is that as perilous as the climb appeared to me, that climb was made daily by the lighthouse keeper to polish the inside and the outside of the lens and to turn the light on so that ships could see it at night and in dense fog. The keepers did everything daily to maintain the lamp's illumination in order to save human lives and precious cargo. As the bearer of light, you remain on call every waking moment. The causes of darkness do not rest, and neither should the light bearer.

Likewise, you are charged every day with the responsibility to climb the wonderful, blessed, and safe steps to the Lord and polish your lenses. When you come to the Lord, you are renewed in mind and in spirit. You are revitalized and made able to preserve precious lives and keep valuable human cargo secure. You get to increase your lumens, by putting on more and more of the Word of God into your life, and working it to achieve deeper understanding day by day. You are also going to live more and more by the Word of God, and not by enticements, temptations or lusts. As a requirement you're going to study in the book of Matthew, Chapters 5—7, the Sermon on the Mount and master it thoroughly, because it is among the best scriptures for learning how to live and maintain a Christian way of life. I challenge you to read those chapters in the book of Matthew and to study and understand every word, every thought and every phrase. This is a sure source for increasing the lumens and brighten the light in your spiritual life.

ALWAYS IN REMEMBRANCE (2 PETER 1:15)

1. Light bearers _____ darkened hearts.
2. Light bearers must polish their lenses _____ by studying the Word of God.
3. Your light can _____ others to salvation and peaceful lives.
4. The _____ in you can be dimmed or extinguished only if you allow it.
5. A light is not lit to be _____ from view.
6. You have been illuminated by the light of _____.

SCRIPTURE REFERENCE:

Matthew 5:13-14, 16; Proverbs 15:1; Mark 9:50; Luke 14:34-35; 1 John 1:5;

Matthew Chapters 5-7

TEN POINTS *of* LIGHT

HIGHER GROUND PRINCIPLE # 13

Let God's light into your heart by relating positively with others.

The Ten Commandments teach us how to have and maintain a relationship with God. The Sermon on the Mount presents Jesus' teachings for us on how to live righteously according to the Gospel doctrine for a Christian life. And now you can learn from the Apostle Peter how to live rightly with men. I've termed this section the Ten Points of Light because there are ten principles that when applied, they shed light into interrelationships with others. When you apply these ten principles, the great light of understanding how to relate with others will be shed into your heart.

Here are the biblical keys for how to get it done, how to overcome the propensity to offend others, and how to minimize or avoid and overcome being offended by others. There are ten points of light in the following passage that give you instruction on how to live godly lives among men.

> Having your conversation honest
> among the Gentiles: that, whereas they
> speak against you as evildoers, they
> may by your good works, which they
> shall behold, glorify God in the day of
> visitation. Submit yourselves to every
> ordinance of man for the Lord's sake:
> whether it be to the king, as supreme;
> Or unto governors, as unto them that
> are sent by him for the punishment of

evildoers, and for the praise of them
that do well. For so is the will of God,
that with well doing ye may put to
silence the ignorance of foolish men:
As free, and not using your liberty for
a cloke of maliciousness, but as the
servants of God. Honour all men. Love
the brotherhood. Fear God. Honour
the king.

1 Peter 2: 12—17

THE TEN POINTS OF LIGHT IN 1PETER

1. Be honest (in everything)
2. Do good works (in every way)
3. Obey all laws and regulations (do not take shortcuts that violate ordinances)
4. Always do the right thing (even if it's not to your favor)
5. Don't use Christianity to beat others down (avoid putting guilt trips on people)
6. Be first a servant of God (Put God first in everything you do)
7. Don't dishonor or disrespect others (put away your airs of superiority)
8. Express love to those in the church family (not just on Sundays when we see each other)
9. Hold God and the things of God in reverential fear (don't compromise your godliness)
10. Honor the elected or appointed heads of state (although you may not agree with them)

1. Be honest (in everything)

If someone comes up with a grand scheme that sounds good because you are going to profit from it, but it is not honest, then it is incumbent upon you to walk away from it. Prosperity derived from unscrupulous means may appear to be fantastic at the time, but soon it will work against you and cause ruin to take root in your life (Proverbs 1:10). Be honest in everything. Just ask yourself, "What would Jesus do?" "Would He do this"? You are obligated to act as Jesus would because you are His representative. Those of you who understand law can appreciate that if you are His agent, you have an agency relationship with Jesus Christ. The things that you commit to here on earth are binding Him who is in Heaven (Matthew 16:19). As an agent of Jesus Christ, you never want to give the wrong impression, or come across as sufficiently vague, enough for someone to misconstrue your intentions. You always want to give the right impression. Being honest is critical to having good relationships with everyone around you.

2. Do good works (in every way)

Don't just say, "I'm going to do this because it is good for this person", when in reality you are doing it for a totally different purpose than to benefit the one in need. Always do good in every way and in everything you do for everyone. There are no exceptions when it comes to doing good. Doing good should become your mantra, as you commit to it to be your unconditional way of life from this day forward. The following is what is required of you in order to do good works: changing your way of life so that you live a godly lifestyle, and letting those lumens of light shine through brighter and brighter. You become saltier and saltier, and you have more and more flavor to season events around you. When somebody licks you, they'll say, "Mmm, this tastes good." I mean this as a figure of speech, not literally. When they have an interaction with you or develop a relationship with you, your light will be shed upon them, and they will desire your company.

3. Obey all laws and regulations (do not take shortcuts that violate ordinances)

Do not take shortcuts if they're in violation of ordinances. When you get to a stop sign, it means stop. That is an ordinance set in place for everyone's wellbeing. It does not mean slow down, and if the coast is clear, roll on through. If you get into the practice of violating what may seem to you as insignificant ordinances for your convenience, and you think that doing less than what is required is okay, the day will come when you'll violate an ordinance at the wrong time and in the wrong place. That's when incrimination lands at your front door. Those who witness your flagrant behavior become justified in their thinking that church people are a bunch of hypocrites, because they do the same as others do. The incident may cost you fines, incarceration, and surely bring on shame. They are going to say, "Oh, and that's a Christian, hmm!" Don't tell me that you haven't had a similar experience at some point in your life. You know that we Bible-carrying Christians are easily identifiable and can be picked out of a crowd by our demeanor of kindness and compassion, and our conversation which is centered around the Word. The Christian is more noticeable when he or she is misbehaving because everyone's eyes are on you waiting for you to slip. When you let yourself slip due to bad habits you built up over time, you are both placing yourself in a precarious position vulnerable to criticism, and causing the ministry to be blamed. (2 Corinthians 6:3).

> Giving no offence in any thing, that the
> ministry be not blamed:
>
> *2 Corinthians 6:3*

This is the opposite effect of what Christians want to have on others. As Christians we are to be blameless and harmless, without fault and shine as lights in the world. (Philippians 2:15). The world should know who you are at all times by your behavior and your compliance with laws, ordinances, and regulations. You cannot just ignore the ordinances and expect to be regarded as a disciple of Christ, especially that you were instructed in Titus 3:1 to obey magistrates. We were once like everyone else, foolish, disobedient, deceived, serving our own pleasures and lusts, living in malice and envy, hateful, and hating one another, but the love of God rescued us out of that prison and set us free by the Holy Spirit and enabled us out of His mercy to be able to resist the evil which through temptations engulf the world.

4. Always do the right thing (even if it's not to your favor)

You are going to be tremendously challenged to always do the right thing, particularly when it's not in your favor. You are constantly facing situations where you might feel that you can get away without having to do the right thing, just this one time. You are commanded to do the right thing all the time! You can't allow yourself to lavish in weakness and give in for convenience. You have to think of the life you live as the thickness of your armor protecting you from deadly blows, and every time that you deviate from this Christian precept you are exposed to another kink in your armor. You know why warriors wear armor. Armor protects from oncoming arrows penetrating the skin. They go "bing" on impact as they bounce off. If the armor takes a blow from a sword, it dents the armor and most likely prevents injury to the body. That's how armor protects, and when you leave your sanctuary, you are to be dressed in the full armor of God (Ephesians 6: 10-17). But every time that you deviate from the Christian walk behaving in ungodly ways, you are saying, "Well, it's probably not a sin if I do it, just this once." Or you may say, "If I don't do the right thing, because they don't really deserve it, then I have not sinned". Well, that's not true. What the Word says is that if you know it is the right thing to do and you refuse to do it, it is sin: "Therefore to him that knoweth to do good, and doeth it not, to him it is sin" (James 4:17). When you fail to do the right thing, you abandon the protection of God's shield over you, and you become vulnerable to the fiery darts of the adversary and the crippling blows of life.

5. Don't use Christianity to beat others down (avoid putting guilt trips on people)

Resist the temptation to use Christianity to beat others down. Employ every bit of mental energy for self control to avoid putting guilt trips on others. We do this to each other. We do this amongst ourselves from friend to friend, and we do this to our family, and it especially occurs in couples, way too often. We often violate the trust our closest friends put in us, and cause our relationships to break down. You may sarcastically say to someone who has faltered, "Well, that's a good Christian example!" Meaning, that was not the Christian thing to do, but the tone is heavy and accusatory, my friend, that is not a blessing anyone is eager to receive. It would be a blessing if you used the incident as a teachable moment to lovingly introduce the brother in Christ to the corresponding scripture to correct his behavior, and to help him comprehend the godly principles involved (2 Timothy 3:16). It is usually someone very close to you that you beat down with the Word. That's the meaning of the phrase, "Not using your liberty for a cloak of maliciousness." You're using the cloak of Christianity to express sarcasm where love should rule being served with kindness. You shouldn't be thinking, "Well, I'm holier than thou," and use that as the premise to beat someone down. That's not the right way to teach Christian principles to others. The way to teach is to demonstrate biblical principles by your application of them, not by making people feel bad or by making them feel inferior. All that is accomplished when you make them feel bad is to turn the person off. Sometimes a believer gets turned off with you for treating them that way, and they may also get turned off to the Word. If you thought you were witnessing to your brother, sister, mother, father, or spouse and you beat them down with the Word; your salt has lost its flavor for that person. If you've ever been beaten down with the Word, you know exactly what I'm talking about; it's not a good feeling, and the mind reels with scenarios for retaliation and other repercussions. If you've ever beaten someone down with the Word, you know that you need to stop doing that, mend the fences you've broken, and you need to just not do that anymore.

6. Be first a servant of God (Put God first in everything you do)

If you find yourself in a situation where you are unsure of what to do, ask yourself, if Jesus Christ were in this position, what would Jesus do? Then do as you know that He would do. If you're not sure, ask Him, because you've got His spirit and He is certain to put the right inspiration in your heart, which is what you need in this instance. The Holy Spirit will communicate and tell you and put the right conviction in your heart. Being first a servant to God requires that you emulate Jesus. He is the only example for you to follow. As a servant of God, you must know what things God requires of you in handling any given situation or circumstance. The conclusion is that you will do what God wants first and foremost, regardless of how much it might conflict with someone else's or your own desire. "What does God want me to do in this situation?" is the best question to ask. If you are not sure, say "Gee, what would Jesus do in a situation like this?" You know that Jesus first sought the Father's guidance, and He never failed to follow the advice and direction from God. Make it a point to read the book of Matthew, Chapters 5 through 7, and in particular study the Sermon on the Mount. You will find that it covers every principle for understanding the importance of putting God first.

7. Don't dishonor or disrespect others (put away your airs of superiority)

The best way for you not to dishonor or disrespect others is to learn and practice honoring and respecting behavior. Disrespect and dishonor of others occurs when you put on airs of superiority or when you, by what you say, make others both intentionally and unintentionally feel that they are inferior, that's being condescending to others, and sets the stage for an unsuccessful relationship. Never allow yourself to utter something that could make another person feel small or to behave in ways that make others look small. That is behavior that causes dishonor and disrespect of others. Assume that everyone knows who you are. For example, if you're the boss, everybody knows both your name and who you are. If they don't know that you are the boss, it's not going to be long before they become aware of this well-known fact. So, you don't need to walk in and say, "Hello, everybody. I'm the boss." They already know you. What they perceive you're saying to them is, "You idiots, don't you know that I'm the boss, and those of you that don't know I'm the boss are a bunch of idiots. I'm telling you that I'm the boss, so now you know, you bunch of idiots." We do the same in many aspects of our lives. If you're the parent, your child knows that you're the parent. You don't have to beat them over the head with the universally accepted fact that you are their mother, or father. Whoever you are in your position in life, everyone who needs to know who you are, already knows who you are. You don't need to lord your title over them. Just be your normal self. Be yourself, cease being obnoxious, pretentious, and putting on airs, and people will grow to respect you. Show respect to others, and earn their respect, as well.

8. Express love to those in the church family (not just on Sundays when we see each other)

Express love to those in the Church family, not only when you get together on Sunday but throughout the week, day-by-day. Every moment presents a new opportunity for you to demonstrate your love. It is up to you to create the opportunity to show your love to someone else. You can show your love to others by staying in contact and by lending your help when it is needed. Say, for example, a brother is ill and needs help with food shopping or picking up a prescription. You would not necessarily know this unless you were involved. You wouldn't be helpful unless you knew that this particular help was needed. I understand that we all love each other, and that's wonderful. I know that if there is anything that any one of us can do for another, we would not hesitate to do it. I know, that you know that, too. But you need to express ongoing love. You can express ongoing love by being in contact with each other on a regular basis, if only just to say hello, to see what you could pray for, or to see how you can be a blessing to that brother or sister. There's nothing wrong with making a "love call" or "love visit." Today, we have text messaging, IM, and several other digital forms of instant communication, as well as cell phones; some of us still have house phones (land lines), we have e-mail, and Alexa; not to mention the old snail mail of the U.S. Postal Service, all these means for staying in touch. You can communicate if you so desire. There's nothing to stop you from communicating with one another. If you're not communicating with another brother in Christ, it means that during the entire week you're not giving yourself the opportunity to bless a brother or sister or to be blessed by a brother or sister. You need to change that way of living. It's one of the keys to living a life full of light to be able to be a blessing, give a blessing, and receive a blessing. Express love to those in the Church family. A great example of brotherly love can be seen in Luke 5:18-19. These men heard that Jesus was in town, and they knew where He would be. They carried their paralytic friend in his bed. When they couldn't get through the crowd to bring him to Jesus, they climbed the roof and let him down in his bed in the midst of Jesus. That kind of determination is only borne out of a deep brotherly love and genuine concern. You can learn to love like that too.

9. Hold God and the things of God in reverential fear (don't compromise your godliness)

Reverential fear is a good term to know, because it is not this shaky kind of fear, associated with the kind of horror one experiences in horror movies or spook houses. It is a fear that comes from knowing that God is omnipotent, and that if He wanted to, He could put an end to all this, right here, right now. We cannot do a thing to stop Him. We cannot change the will of God (Numbers 16:31—33). What God has put into motion will stay in motion until He brings it to a halt, no man can alter the course of the path set by God. Not one of us can change what God has ordained. You have to express reverential awe for who the Almighty God is. Your heart should cry out intensely, "God, I want to do your will. God, I want to respect your things, I want to fulfill the things that you've asked of me. I want to obey you because You are God and I am Your servant as well as Your child. But I am first in a relationship of being a servant to do Your will, and then I'm in a relationship with You as Your child." Your choice is obvious, though limited. You have free will, and you can choose not to do as God ordains, but to not do His will is the worse choice you can make; it's not a good choice (Luke 12:5). The Father has chosen you to be an integral part of His family, a family that is full of hope, compassion and love; the kind you will find nowhere on earth. Father God, YAHWEH, is to be revered.

10. Honor the elected or appointed heads of state (although you may not agree with them)

Sometimes you look at the people who are running the government and say, "Where did they come from?" You may think that you could do a better job, but you are not the one who was elected. You are not the one who was appointed. But you have a responsibility, if you want to live a peaceful life, and that is to bring honor to the heads of state. You choose to honor the heads of state, not because they deserve it, not because they earned it, and not because you're forced to agree with them, but because God tells you that if you are to live a peaceful life, this is what you must do. Honor the elected and appointed heads of state. Just as God works with you and through you to accomplish His purpose, God may just as well be working to accomplish His will through those officials whom you are so disappointed in. You don't know what God is up to with respect to how He uses anyone. For the most part, we are not sure of exactly how He is using us. We should pray for our officials, and we should honor them, as well.

The ten precepts described above are like ten points of light. Obey these ten rules in order to live a peaceful life and to shed light into the darkness of the world. If not, you are not part of the solution but part of the problem. You don't want to be found to have been in that position when the Lord returns. John 15:8 reads, "Herein is my Father glorified, that you bear much fruit." God is glorified when you bear fruit. "So shall you be my disciples." Not only is God glorified when you bear fruit in your life, but that fruit is how you are identified as a disciple of Jesus Christ.

So what does it mean to bear fruit? To bear fruit in your life, in the context that is spoken of here, is to bring godliness into your life and into the life of others. It really is a simple precept to understand especially in light of Galatians 5:22—23, which spells out the fruit of the spirit. Are you bringing godliness into your life? Are you bringing godliness into the situation that you are in at work, at home, or wherever you happen to be?

If you are not, you are not glorifring God, if you are, you are glorifring God. You are bearing fruit, and your identity is that of a disciple of Jesus.

The scripture further tells us in John 8:9-11 that "As the Father has loved me, so have I loved you; continue ye in my love. If you keep my commandments, you shall abide in my love, even as I have kept my Father's commandments and abide in his love. These things I have spoken unto you, that my joy might remain in you, and that your joy may be full."

Are you full of joy? Yes? Good! If you are not, then please go back and review the ten principles referenced above, for they describe the things needed for filling your life to the brim and overflowing with joy. If you are full of joy, you need to continue in those precepts to maintain a life filled with joy. God makes it so simple for you, doesn't He? Now that you have the correct and proper recipe for a joy filled life, you can see that it is fairly easy to do and to sustain throughout your life. You will want to continue being the salt o the earth, because if you are not the salt, you are useless. If you lose your flavor, you are not good to anyone. You have to maintain your flavor. You also have to be that shining bright light in the darkness of the world around you. If you cover that light, that is, intermittently not living godly and occasionally failing to take your witness and testimony of Christ in you to world, then you are just not living up to God's expectation of you. That's the way you should think about the Lord's calling, so that you always have the presence of mind to meet God's expectation of you, as its fulfilled day by day. That is why He has given you all these wonderful tools to work with; love joy, peace, patience, longsuffering, kindness gentleness, faith, goodness, meekness, and self-control. He says, "Now that I have given you the tools to work with, this is what I expect you to do. Now go and live up to it". If you do as He has asked, you will notice things start to turn to the positive side rather quickly; conflict will dissipate out of your life. I'm not saying that everybody else is going to do the right thing for you. That should not be your expectation. What it assures is that you will be walking with the Holy Spirit. He shall not forsake or allow you to be tempted more than what you are able to handle. The expectation is that you do the right things according to the high calling that God has called you to, and you place yourself in the hands of the Lord and leave the results up to Him.

ALWAYS IN REMEMBRANCE: 2 PETER 1:15

1. Be _____ in everything.
2. Do _____ works in every way.
3. _____ all laws and regulations.
4. Always work to meet God's _____.
5. Don't _____ Christianity to beat others down.
6. Be _____ a servant of God.
7. Don't dishonor or _____ others.
8. Express _____ to the Church family.
9. _____ God in reverential fear.
10. _____ the elected and appointed heads ofstate.

SCRIPTURE REFERENCE:

Matthew Chapters 5—7; 1 Peter 2: 12—17; James 4:17; John 15:8; John 8:9—11;

Proverbs 1:10; Matthew 5:19; 2 Corinthians 6:3; Philippians 2:15; Titus 3:1;

Ephesians 6:10-17; 2 Timothy 3:16; Luke 5:18-19; Numbers 16:31-33;

Luke 12:5; Galatians 5:22-23

X.

HANDLING THOSE
WHO OFFEND YOU

HIGHER GROUND PRINCIPLE # 14

Follow the example of forgiveness
given by Jesus.

You thirst, as I do, for proper instruction on right daily living, and especially in moments of crisis or events that evoked ill thoughts. Meanwhile, the Bible's instruction is staring you right in the face. But you are reluctant to accept the instruction at the moment because it does not align with the heightened emotions urging you to respond from your old preconceived ideals of what is just, moral, ethical, or right. Anger can be overwhelming and it can sway you into choosing the wrong set of precepts that yield the most satisfaction in that moment of anger. Be sober, be vigilant because the adversary, like a roaring lion walks about seeking who he can devour. (1Peter 5:8). In this scenario your anger has turned you into fresh red meat for the adversary. To avoid being victimized you have to prepare in advance, to first recognize the attacks from the devil, and second, to know how to resist him. Temptation will never go away, so you have to be prepared with the correct biblical principles to apply in any given situation. Being prepared to take the initiative requires that you practice daily applying the biblical precepts in your dealings with others, so you can recognize when others are not applying the same precepts when dealing with you. Each of us is tempted with the thought of being the exception to God's rules from time to time, especially when His rules oppose the activity or lifestyle you long to engage in. Why do you think you're tempted to think this way? Where did you get the idea that you merit or have earned such a privilege to be exempted from God's rules? It most certainly did not come from God, so you need a closer examination of the source of your motives. Consider what you have been doing recently, or habitually do that may be stimulating you away from godly behavior and desiring ungodly ways.

The Bible tells us that we were saved (redeemed) when we were in our worst state; dead in trespasses and sin. You were condemned to death, but Jesus took your place at the gallows and died in our place (Isaiah 53:5). If anything, you are the debtor to Him for His substitution for you at Calvary. Jesus died on the cross to provide you freedom from the chains of temptation and sin. That is the strength that you will have when you choose to resist the devil. You have an advocate who showed you the strength of His will to obey the Father, to the end of dying for you.

No person can claim what was given at Calvary unless they have truly accepted Jesus as Lord and are doing His will of their own free will, by free choice, and by obedience. (*Matthew 7:21—23*)

In effect, we are without excuse not to be 100 percent obedient to the precepts set by God. He sent His Son to teach us and show us how to obey God's will for man, and He purchased mankind back by sacrificing the life of His only begotten Son. It wasn't just death, it was a torturous and painful death that Jesus endured as He gave His life in payment for all of man's wrong doing, and paid the price so that mankind could return to God. Consider these two things being asked of you in return.

> But I say unto you, That whosoever is
> angry with his brother without a cause
> shall be in danger of the judgment: and
> whosoever shall say to his brother, Raca,
> shall be in danger of the council: but
> whosoever shall say, Thou fool, shall
> be in danger of hell fire. Therefore if
> thou bring thy gift to the altar, and

there rememberest that thy brother hath
ought against thee; Leave there thy gift
before the altar, and go thy way; first
be reconciled to thy brother, and then
come and offer thy gift. Agree with
thine adversary quickly, whiles thou art
in the way with him; lest at any time
the adversary deliver thee to the judge,
and the judge deliver thee to the officer,
and thou be cast into prison. Verily I
say unto thee, Thou shalt by no means
come out thence, till thou hast paid the
uttermost farthing.

Matthew 5:22—26

1. Be reconciled to your brother.
2. Agree with your adversary quickly.

These are two specific instructions directly from the Lord that teach you how to handle conflict with others. Do not assume that you are okay with God while you have an unresolved conflict with a brother in Christ. The modern-day Christian believes that if they forgive the person, that is sufficient, and they are right with God again. Yes, forgiveness is a requirement, but you must take note that the scripture says, " first be reconciled to thy brother". Your responsibility is to clean up the relationship and then come to God with a pure and clean heart. Most of us don't enjoy being in a state of conflict with others, but some languish in it and refuse to put away their pride. Pride prevents them from dealing with their error. This is a carnal state of the mind, and when the mind is unwilling to change, the Word says that the mind is reprobate (2 Corinthians 13:5-7). You are not instructed to go and straighten out the other person. Rather, you are told to straighten out yourself by reconciling, for these two reasons:

1. So that your offerings are acceptable to God.

God prefers obedience over sacrifices. (1 Samuel 15:22). If you fail or refuse to change your mind concerning those with whom you have conflict, then you are disobedient to God's instruction. This example is prevalent in married men who dishonor their wives and cause their prayers to be hindered. (1 Peter 3:7).

2. To avoid real big problems with secular authorities.

God is merciful and extends His mercy to the meek and humble. When you are prideful and decide to take matters into your own hands, you take God out of the picture and cast yourself into the bands of the rulers of the world. You become subject to their ungodly and unjust ways. By settling the matter quickly, you remain humble and in fellowship with God.

God's disposition on offenses to you or by you is best reflected in the following verses in Matthew 18. He will not tolerate your misbehavior, nor will He tolerate others' mistreatment of His little ones. God has appointed Angels to watch over His people, and they have instant access to God if they need to intervene for God's people.

Woe unto the world because of offenses!
For it must needs be that offenses come;
but woe to that man by whom the
offense cometh! Wherefore if thy hand
or thy foot offend thee, cut them off,
and cast them from thee: it is better for
thee to enter into life halt or maimed,
rather than having two hands or two
feet to be cast into everlasting fire.
And if thine eye offend thee, pluck it
out, and cast it from thee: it is better

for thee to enter into life with one eye,
rather than having two eyes to be cast
into hell fire. Take heed that ye despise
not one of these little ones; for I say
unto you, That in heaven their angels
do always behold the face of my Father
which is in heaven.

Matthew 18:7-10

ALWAYS IN REMEMBRANCE: 2 PETER 1:15

3. You were _____ from sin and death while you were in your worst state.

4. You thirst for instruction on _____ daily living.

5. Before worshipping God, you should first be _____ with your partner.

6. You should _____ with an adversary quickly.

7. You are to _____ out yourself so that your offerings are acceptable to God.

8. You are to agree quickly with adversaries to _____ bigger issues with secular authorities.

SCRIPTURE REFERENCE:

Matthew 5:22—26; 2 Corinthians 13:5—7; Matthew 18:7—10; 1 Peter 5:8; Isaiah 53:5;

Matthew 7:21-23; Matthew 25:22-26; 1 Samuel 15:22; 1 Peter 3:7

XI.

Handling Quarrels among Christians

HIGHER GROUND PRINCIPLE # 15

Avoid quarrels; do not trespass against others.

Moreover if thy brother shall trespass
against thee, go and tell him his fault
between thee, and him alone: if he shall
hear thee, thou hast gained thy brother.

Matthew 18:15-17

What does it mean for your brother or sister to trespass against you? A trespass is a major violation of exercising your will over another without regard for their rights or feelings. In a relationship, many opportunities arise daily to commit trespasses against each other. There are many types of trespasses, but we will examine only a few in order to shed light and increase our understanding of what is being communicated in the Bible on this topic.

Here is what God's Word defines as trespasses we commit against each other:

1. Grieves your soul—makes you feel emotional illness.
2. Affronts you—causes painful confrontation and provokes an ill response.
3. Abuses you—unfair bullying; someone who is more eloquent, talks louder, or uses an economic, emotional or personal advantage over you to get their way.
4. Gossips and besmirches your standing among others in the Church—brings false accusations, tale-bearing, tattle-telling.
5. Is injurious to your estate—puts you down.

An exhortation from the Word is that you take the initiative to draw a person's attention to your feelings if he or she commits a trespass against you. Our tendency is to sulk and harbor ill feelings until the person voluntarily comes around and apologizes, or time passes and you don't feel as aggrieved. You may try sending subtle messages by mistreating them or ignoring them until they come around, but that doesn't usually work, instead it may escalate the problem. Worse yet, sometimes we send an envoy through the person's close friends to carry our message of hurt. These messengers are often ill-equipped and not necessarily delicate in their delivery. The end result is that a situation that might have been easily resolved gets escalated to a stage where friendships and relationships are put in jeopardy. Such errors should not be committed, since you know that the spiritual solution is for you to go alone and tell him/her their fault between you and them. If he hears your point of view and appreciates what has transpired, you will gain their respect, and the relationship will be healed and preserved, and may even attain greater heights.

Nonetheless, if the other person has a lesser understanding of godly principles than you do, you might exercise greater caution in your approach so that they do not perceive it as an unprovoked confrontation. In such cases, you must use a didactic approach to teach the biblical principle before you bring up the fault. Otherwise, the uninstructed person may be offended and pushed away inadvertently due to their error, thinking that you are treating them unfairly.

> And through thy knowledge shall
> the weak brother perish, for whom
> Christ died? But when ye sin so against
> the brethren, and wound their weak
> conscience, ye sin against Christ.
> Wherefore, if meat make my brother
> to offend, I will eat no flesh while the
> world standeth, lest I make my brother
> to offend.

1 Corinthians 8: 11-13

Doing something to exploit another person's lesser understanding of God's Word or lesser ability regarding spiritual matters, or compelling another to sin through their weakness, is a sin. You must guard that you are not the source of such a provocation of another to sin. This issue is speaking to your misappropriation of the Word principles, or going outside of the Word, which makes you the one who commits the offense against a brother. In such instances when you've caused someone else to sin, you too have sinned. The reminder is for you, when you are the aggrieved, to abstain from doing things that would offend others and abstain from offending others in order to achieve your own vain and self-indulgent satisfaction of giving them a piece of your mind. If a partner or ssociate offends you, you need to go back and review Matthew 18 for instruction on how to overcome and get past any anger or desire for revenge without sinning.

> But why dost thou judge thy brother?
> or why dost thou set at nought thy
> brother? for we shall all stand before
> the judgment seat of Christ. For it is
> written, As I live, saith the Lord, every

knee shall bow to me, and every tongue
shall confess to God. So then every
one of us shall give account of himself
to God. Let us not therefore judge one
another any more: but judge this rather,
that no man put a stumblingblock or an
occasion to fall in his brother's way.

Romans 14:10-13

And the King shall answer and say unto
them, Verily I say unto you, Inasmuch
as ye have done it unto one of the least
of these my brethren, ye have done it
unto me.

Matthew 25:40

The Bible is very specific about God's view of men when it comes to offending one another. We are boldly reminded that we all will stand before the Lord, at the judgment seat of Christ, to give account for your every action. There is no escape from this for anyone. You should take the initiative in your relationship not to be offensive or judgmental of others so that you are not held accountable on the day of judgment. The Lord reminds us that offending even the least of these, His brethren, is the same as offending Him. The scriptures are replete in expressing this principle. Even the Law of Moses was not silent concerning matters between the brethren. The following passages are enlightening when considering God's point of view on handling conflict in your relationship.

And the LORD spake unto Moses,
saying, If a soul sin, and commit a
trespass against the LORD, and lie
unto his neighbour in that which was

delivered him to keep, or in fellowship,
or in a thing taken away by violence, or
hath deceived his neighbour; Or have
found that which was lost, and lieth
concerning it, and sweareth falsely;
in any of all these that a man doeth,
sinning therein: Then it shall be,
because he hath sinned, and is guilty,
that he shall restore that which he took
violently away, or the thing which he
hath deceitfully gotten, or that which
was delivered him to keep, or the lost
thing which he found, Or all that about
which he hath sworn falsely; he shall
even restore it in the principal, and shall
add the fifth part more thereto, and give
it unto him to whom it appertaineth, in
the day of his trespass offering.

Leviticus 6: 1-5

Thou shalt not defraud thy neighbour,
neither rob him: the wages of him that
is hired shall not abide with thee all
night until the morning. Thou shalt
not curse the deaf, nor put a stumbling
block before the blind, but shalt fear
thy God: I am the LORD. Ye shall do
no unrighteousness in judgment: thou
shalt not respect the person of the poor,
nor honour the person of the mighty:
but in righteousness shalt thou judge
thy neighbour. Thou shalt not go up
and down as a talebearer among thy
people: neither shalt thou stand against

the blood of thy neighbour: I am the
LORD. Thou shalt not hate thy brother
in thine heart: thou shalt in any wise
rebuke thy neighbour, and not suffer sin
upon him. Thou shalt not avenge, nor
bear any grudge against the children
of thy people, but thou shalt love thy
neighbour as thyself: I am the LORD.

Leviticus 19: 13-18

When that Christian brother (your sister, wife, husband, friend, child, parent, employer, employee, or someone else) does offend you, you are not to let your displeasure fester into a secret malicious plot to get even or weave a plan with which to bring him down. You should first make a substitution for him. Put yourself in his place; which is what Christ did for you. Think about what this person might be going through at the moment, and don't dwell so much on how hurt your feelings are. Have a compassionate attitude instead of an insulted attitude. Then, do as Matthew 18:15 instructs, Go and tell him his fault... We usually stop reading right here. There is no period after fault. You are not told to go and tell him off. You are told to discuss the matter privately with him.

Your relationships can improve substantially if you put more of Christ and less of yourself into your thinking and handling of issues that arise. You may first want to take inventory of your own shortcomings. For example, consider how you respond to things and how you perceive others, any inbred attitudes from your childhood and upbringing that are different from your partner's. Remember that you are each made differently and uniquely. Couple that with your unique set of life experiences and how different they may have been for someone else and you will not find anyone identical to you. In fact, someone else in the same circumstance may not have perceived the experience or come to the same conclusion as you. Being patient and understanding instead of angry, insulted, and judgmental, is the best approach to solving problems that arise in your relationship.

ALWAYS IN REMEMBRANCE: 2 PETER 1:15

1. When someone offends you, it _____ your soul and makes you feel emotional illness.
2. An affront causes painful confrontation and _____ an ill response.
3. Abuse and unfair _____ occurs when someone uses their talents to take advantage of others.
4. Gossip is a root for false _____ of others.
5. Tale-bearing is _____ and puts the other person down.
6. Tattle-telling is very _____ to the victim.

SCRIPTURE REFERENCE:

Matthew 18:15—17; 1 Corinthians 8:11—13; Romans 14:10—13;

Matthew 25:40; Leviticus 6:1—5; Leviticus 19: 13—18

Maintaining Good Relationships:

HIGHER GROUND PRINCIPLE # 16

Maintain peace, love, and joy in the Church and in your relationship.

In this section, we want to expound on preserving purity and holiness in the Church. A problem that arises in the Church is that sometimes we are trying to maintain good relationships with each other by applying the standards of the world (Gr. aion = 'this age'), applying the definition of the world to define the Christian relationship. You must be careful to be obedient to and apply biblical principles in defining your relationships. The world is not your friend; it is your enemy. Therefore, any behavior according to the world is contrary to the better good of the Church. In fact, anything in your life that is not of, or from God, only serves to work against you, even if you don't realize it at the time (Romans 12:2).

The Word calls you to maintain peace, love, and joy within the Church, against such there is no law. Regarding everyone else outside the Church, you simply want to come to the quickest and easiest resolution so that you don't get entangled in situations that spiral out of control. In the Church, you are charged to forgive and to bring peace between you and your brethren.

You must be sure that your personal relationships are devoid of sarcasm, conflict, and abrasive behavior, as is common, expected and largely accepted behavior outside the church. You can avoid these undesirable characteristics by changing your attitude, if it is a confronting attitude, and pursuing a gentler and kinder approach. Perhaps you put yourself in your partner's place or sacrifice your point of view until the crisis blows over. Outright accusations are discouraged, because they evoke angry and defensive responses.

Remember that the only thing you can control in a confrontation is' yourself. You can keep from railing accusations and driving the conversation further into the negative. At some point in the discussion, it is more prudent to stay quiet and let the other person vent. Hopefully, their tirade will be short-lived, and if there is ranting that might otherwise incite or spark a negative response from you, you have prepared yourself to allow it to pass. It's imperative to keep your emotions in check at all times to maintain harmony in the relationship.

A gentle answer turns away wrath, but a
harsh word stirs up anger.

Proverbs 15:1 NASB

ALWAYS IN REMEMBRANCE: 2 PETER 1:15

7. No one likes a confronting _____.

8. It is best to let the other person _____ down.

9. Railing accusations cause others to become _____ and they either attack or clam up.

10. Be in _____ of your emotions when you approach a brother to resolve a matter.

11. The only perfect one is _____.

12. A _____ answer turns away wrathful anger.

SCRIPTURE REFERENCE:

Romans 12:2; Proverbs 15:1

XII.

The Witness *of the* Church

HIGHER GROUND PRINCIPLE #17

Be a winner in every situation.

Who would not like to win every argument? Today, you're going to learn how God designed it for you never to lose an argument.

> But if he will not hear thee, then take
> with thee one or two more, that in the
> mouth of two or three witnesses every
> word may be established.

Matthew 18:16

The charge to the Christian is to be a peacemaker. This is so ifferent from what you have learned in life. Being a peacemaker is different from the behavior you have observed from those around you. The model in your legacy is reacting as emotions dictate in the heat of a confrontation. You are a captive of wrong thinking. The right thinking is to get past all the emotional fluff and hang-ups and to get back on track with your fellowship with the Lord. The Word says that your prayers are hindered when you approach God while at odds with your spouse (1 Peter 3:7), and that your offerings are not acceptable to God when you are in contention with others (Matthew 5:23—24). Can anything in the Bible be any clearer than this, regarding how you are to live a holy and blessed life? After all, the two great commandments are to love God with all your heart, soul, and mind, and to love others as you love yourself (Matthew 22:36—40).

So, there you stand, aggrieved, having tried discussing the matter privately one-on one with the vilan, only to be rejected. What are you to do? Verse 16 in Matthew 22 does not instruct you to give up on this brother or to go tell everyone else your side of the story behind his back. To the contrary, it exhorts you to continue to resolve the matter privately in a series of progressive escalation. The next step is to take two or three witnesses to make certain that the words spoken are earnest and sincere toward resolving the matter, for the benefit of the individual and for the benefit of the Church by preserving peace and purity in the Church.

You must rise to a higher calling than the other guy, or even higher than you have thought yourself to be. You have been charged with the responsibility to rectify the matter, and you were provided a set of progressive instructions for getting it done the right way, as a blessing to the parties involved and preserving the unity of the Church. That may seem unfair given that your feelings were hurt, but any other approach would result in one person winning and the other losing, both persons losing, and the Church divided. Do you want your partner to be a loser? No, of course not. This person might have been your spouse, your friend, or, if there is no other way to describe them, this person is your brother or sister in Christ. This person is an equal heir in eternity with you and with Christ. If all else fails, you are to forgive and continue in prayer so that you are not burdened with the guilt and sin the situation brings. You are a winner because you have stayed the course, aligned with Christ, and you have been the hope for healing in your relationship. Now, that's being a winner.

ALWAYS IN REMEMBRANCE: 2 PETER 1:15

1. Christians are charged to be _____.
2. We are _____ of wrong thinking.
3. Right _____ is tracking in fellowship with the Lord.
4. A man's prayers _____ when there remain unresolved issues with wives.
5. Our offerings are not _____ to God when we are in contention with others.
6. We are to _____ others as we love ourselves.
7. One responds to a misunderstanding by first _____ it with the other person.
8. There is a specified escalation in the Church by which to _____ a conflict.
9. The Word prescribes having two or three _____ along to discuss the matter after meeting privately.
10. Resolving conflicts quickly preserves _____ in the Church.

SCRIPTURE REFERENCE:

Matthew 18:16; 1 Peter 3:7; Matthew 5:23-24; Matthew 22:16, 36-40

THE CONCEPT *of a* WITNESS

HIGHER GROUND PRINCIPLE # 18

Find a qualified Christian to help resolve a matter.

Whoso killeth any person, the murderer
shall be put to death by the mouth of
witnesses: but one witness shall not
testify against any person to cause
him to die.

Numbers 35:30

A witness is a powerful source to rely on for conviction. The Bible speaks to the severity of this by requiring that there be no less than two witnesses who speak forth on a matter. For that reason, the character of the witness always comes into question, presuming that a witness should be one of good character, honest, and of integrity. In the Church, there are many individuals who can assist in resolving a matter between believers, but there are many more who are not qualified and whose character should be questioned before being inserted into conflict resolution. You do not want to turn your personal issues over to those who are uninstructed or inexperienced in counseling lest they cause you to lose objectivity and arrive at wrong conclusions that hurt the relationship rather than restore it. When bringing forth a matter that occurred in public, if there is to be any witnesses, there should be at least two objective and uninterested parties brought forth. Witnesses should only be utilized in the most severe of circumstances and as a matter of last resort for clarifying varying contentions and different views of the incident. The practice of involving witnesses is not recommended unless absolutely necessary since it tends toward escalation of the issue and broadening the number of people involved.

> At the mouth of two witnesses, or three
> witnesses, shall he that is worthy of
> death be put to death; but at the mouth
> of one witness he shall not be put to
> death. The hands of the witnesses shall
> be first upon him to put him to death,
> and afterward the hands of all the
> people. So thou shalt put the evil away
> from among you.

Deuteronomy 17:6-7

I wanted to examine in the verse above the question of integrity of the witnesses. Such persons must be so sure of what they are attesting to that the law requires them to be the first to strike the accused in the case of conviction worthy of a death sentence. Consider before you agree to be a witness for someone else that in God's view your hand is the first to fall upon the accused. Other scriptures on witnesses include the following:

> It is also written in your law, that the
> testimony of two men is true. I am one
> that bear witness of myself, and the Father
> that sent me beareth witness of me.

John 8:17-18

> This is the third time I am coming
> to you. In the mouth of two or three
> witnesses shall every word be established.

2 Corinthians 13: 1

Dare any of you, having a matter against
another, go to law before the unjust,
and not before the saints? Do ye not
know that the saints shall judge the
world? and if the world shall be judged
by you, are ye unworthy to judge the
smallest matters? Know ye not that we
shall judge angels? how much more
things that pertain to this life? If then ye
have judgments of things pertaining to
this life, *set them to judge 'Who are least
esteemed in the church.* I speak to your
shame. Is it so, that there is not a wise
man among you? no, not one that shall
be able to judge between his brethren?
But brother goeth to law with brother,
and that before the unbelievers. Now
therefore there is utterly a fault among
you, because ye go to law one with
another. *Why do ye not rather take wrong?
why do ye not rather suffer yourselves to
be defrauded?* Nay, ye do wrong, and
defraud, and that your brethren.

1 Corinthians 6: 1-8

There is an alternative spoken of here; that is, why not drop the entire
matter. Why suffer more contention and disruption in your life over a single
matter, especially one that pits you against another believer, and particularly
if it's someone you have a relationship with? Going to secular courts puts you
in greater jeopardy, for the world is less sympathetic to obtaining an equitable
solution for the benefit of all, but instead it promotes judgement for one
side winner and the other the loser. In the Church, even the least esteemed

is better qualified to judge than the most competent secular judge, and if these judges were to adjudicate in the Church, they would still be the least esteemed as qualified to judge among believers, in the Church.

The witnesses are to be two or three disinterested parties, persons of some renown and respectability who can also reason the situation impartially with the opponent. Ideally, other believers or elders in the Church would make the best candidates to choose from. Do not take your posse or best friends who are coming along to stick up for you, and anything else you may attempt to do, keep your family out of it. A brother in the Church is more likely to listen to reason from others than from you at this particular cross road. Let the witnesses be both arbitrators and keepers of mental record of the proceedings. You don't need notes or transcripts to be kept of the proceedings, as they would serve no useful purpose after the matter is resolved. But wait, what if the brother refuses to listen to reason from the witnesses? Can you give him your peace of mind and tell him off, then? No!

And if he shall neglect to hear them, tell
it unto the church: but if he neglect to
hear the church, let him be unto thee as
an heathen man and a publican.

Matthew 18:17

There is yet another step that needs to be taken: bring the matter to the Church. This does not mean you get out on the pulpit and tell the congregation what an awful person your adversary is. In fact, any time there is a dispute between two persons, the matter should be handled privately among the fewest number of people possible. In the Church, this is of prime importance, because it resists the forces of division within and among the members of the Church. Remember that in the Church we want to aspire for peace, unity, and purity.

To tell it to the Church is to bring the matter privately to an elder or to the pastor. When a respected elder or the pastor applies the principles of the Word to the matter (2 Timothy 3: 16-17), and if the person refuses to resolve it, then he is to be to you as are other people who are outside the Church. At this point, we are no longer talking about arbitrating the matter. We are speaking about you addressing your obedience to God's Word by the renewing of your mind and refreshing of your soul. You need to have your heart cleansed and find new conviction as the Word of God ministers to your soul. The conviction you are to seek is for God's blessing into your adversary's life so that his heart may change and a blessing be received to prosper the two of you.

Treating him as a heathen or tax collector is an interesting concept worthy of further discussion. Some have argued that this means you are now free to take this person to the authorities to keep him from causing you further harm or to recover losses or damages under civil law. Others contend that it means you should break off any friendship or closeness with this person and cease any further dealings with him. These certainly are appealing arguments, or they could be acceptable compromises, but I have not found a biblical basis that supports such reasoning.

Remember, we are to apply biblical principles to achieve godly living, and we are to be like Christ. What would He have done in a situation like this? What does the Word say? It tells us to treat the person as we would a stranger, and the Word provides the recipe for the treatment of strangers.

> Thou shalt neither vex a stranger, nor
> oppress him: for ye were strangers in the
> land of Egypt.
>
> *Exodus 22:21*

> Let brotherly love continue. Be not
> forgetful to entertain strangers: for
> thereby some have entertained
> angels unawares.
>
> *Hebrews 13: 1-2*

In these words, there is tremendous power and authority given into your hands. What if you had the power and authority to throw this person who has harmed you in prison? Wouldn't you want to give him what he has coming to him? Of course, you would. That is your old nature at work, to get even and extract vengeance by your own or whatever other means. But let us consider God's justice.

> Brethren, if any of you do err from the
> truth, and one convert him; Let him
> know, that he which converteth the
> sinner from the error of his way shall
> save a soul from death, and shall hide a
> multitude of sins.

James 5:19-20

> Verily I say unto you, Whatsoever ye
> shall bind on earth shall be bound in
> heaven: and whatsoever ye shall loose on
> earth shall be loosed in heaven. Again
> I say unto you, That if two of you shall
> agree on earth as touching any thing
> that they shall ask, it shall be done for
> them of my Father which is in heaven.
> For where two or three are gathered
> together in my name, there am I in the
> midst of them.

Matthew 18:18-20

The Lord vested much power and authority in you. You can bind (like entering into a contract) in His name or commit to something on His behalf, and He will honor your call in Heaven. He also wants you to be in agreement with others around you. He says that in the company of two or three, when you ask in His name, His Father shall do it. Consider that God's purpose is to achieve salvation for as many people as possible, and Jesus's endeavor is to get as many as possible through the gates into the Kingdom of God for His Father. With this understanding in your grasp, do you remain inclined to think that God has in any way given you the latitude to inflict harm on another person? He would prefer that you pray for others to seek repentance and that you forgive and look past each other's faults. The Lord has entrusted you with great responsibility and that's why He asks much of you. The tenderness and understanding you show to those who've harmed you complies with the Lord's expectation. The believer's trust in God extends to Him either making restitution for you, or bringing you comfort and peace over every circumstance. God has given you so much, salvation, hope, eternal life; to name but a few, He has every right to expect from you than from any other, to comply with His commands. He forgave your sin, the cost of which is death, and you are expected to likewise, forgive others who trespass against you.

> But he that knew not, and did commit
> things worthy of stripes, shall be beaten
> with few stripes. For unto whomsoever
> much is given, of him shall be much
> required: and to whom men have
> committed much, of him they will ask
> the more.

Luke 12:48

ALWAYS IN REMEMBRANCE: 2 PETER 1:15

1. A matter can be _____ altogether if one so desires.
2. Going to secular court puts you in grave _____.
3. Respectable Church members of renown can reason _____ with both parties.
4. An aggrieved person is more likely to listen to _____ from others.
5. Resolving a matter between brethren offsets the forces _____ in the Church.
6. Telling it to the Church is to _____ the matter to the pastor or an elder.
7. We are to _____ biblical principles to achieve godly living.
8. You should _____ for forgiveness and repentance of any who cause you harm.

SCRIPTURE REFERENCE:

Numbers 35:30; Deuteronomy 17:6—7; John 8:17—18; 2 Corinthians 13:1;

1 Corinthians 6:1—8; Matthew 18:17; Exodus 22:21; Hebrews; 13:1—2;

James 5:19—20; Matthew 18:18—20; Proverbs 11:14; Luke 12:48; 2
    Timothy 3:16-17

XIII.

Constraints *for* Relationships *on* Finances

HIGHER GROUND PRINCIPLE #19

Lord, free me from the love of $money and
chain my heart to loving you and to loving
my brother.

"A friend in need is a friend indeed"

(Author unknown. This saying is not
taken from the Bible).

Finances have probably led to the ruin of relationships more than
anything else, and caused more dissent and division in the Church
than have issues associated with sex, although the topic of sex being
more salacious gets the headlines every time. Money is the popular term
for describing the management of finances in relationships. In general,
people are willing to compromise on most things, but not so much on
their $money. (I've used the term **"$Money"** to signify the illicit love of
money and to differentiate it from the functional purpose of money as the
currency for exchange of goods that is not tied to sin.) $Money is a root
that springs from deep within the fiber of our society and is used as the
chief measure for one's ability to survive, thrive, and enjoy life's pleasures at

their leisure. It is a symbol of wealth and status. $Money is the irresistible magnetic force that compels you to do strange things, often contrary to your better judgment and contrary to your walk of faith. The end result of our romance with $money usually concludes in disappointment, breakups, financial disaster, and in some cases incarceration for criminal acts to obtain or retain money, and from hiding it from the authorities.

> For the love of money is the root of all
> evil: which while some coveted after, they
> have erred from the faith, and pierced
> themselves through with many sorrows.

1 Timothy 6:10

Our sense of $money is to want more of it and to fight to keep what we have, because it provides us with a sense of security and independence. $Money creates a passionate sense of comfort and security centered on the power to buy with cash or credit the things that validate social status. If you stop and think about it, the ill effects of $Money cause many burdensome consequences. The message we convey to each other is that $Money measures the value of human worth, that it sets a standard of measure for comparison of one over another, in accordance to how one measures up financially. This line of thinking works against the foundation of a Christian's walk. As a believer your hope and trust for supplying your needs should be place solely in God. I'm not pretending that in our society money is not important, but I am saying that it should not be the most important thing for you; that's God's place, being the most important thing. There is a balance to be found between the love for $Money and the necessity to have money in order to transact for your needs.

In this segment, we will examine the effect of $Money on the relationship, and how to best relate to others in your life when it comes to money and finances. This issue is pervasive and runs deep into the way of life. The love of $Money causes you to become single focused, and it dilutes fulfillment in the opportunity to value one another on the same terms as the Lord Jesus values us. In a relationship, your partner should be more important than $Money. The quality of the time you spend together should not be watered down because your focus is first on getting more $Money, keeping your $Money safe, than it is on your partner's emotional comfort.

Overcoming Love of $Money

Everyone who covets their relationship with $money has a misplaced sense of love and loyalty. Money is the means for satisfying needs for yourself and for your family, there is no question about that. It is the means that you employ to get money, and the extent to which you will go to for $Money that is of concern. If you replace your reliance on God's ability, willingness and desire to supply your needs with reliance on $money, cash you have in the bank, securities you've invested in, real estate you own, or credit you've secured in credit cards, then the belief that $money can buy you everything will engulf you, and steal your heart from God. You are flawed in your expectation for deliverance, and you put the relationship with your family and your eternal life in jeopardy. God, in His ever-knowing wisdom, identified the tendency for man to love $money as a fault and offered a way to overcome this enslaving predicament with $money.

> And all the tithe of the land, whether
> of the seed of the land, or of the fruit of
> the tree, is the LORD's: it is holy unto
> the LORD.

Leviticus 27:30

In making the declaration that the first tenth of all belongs to Him, God sets in place a pattern to release man from the bondage and sin of covetousness over $money. If you begin to pattern yourself after the commandment from God, and to teach your children the habit of giving that first ten percent of their increase, the value of the remaining ninety percent will be multiplied. You will build a mental barrier of separation from money that later in life will prevent you from becoming obsessed with the love of $money. Your faithful obligation is to honor God by meeting His every requirement, tithing being among the highest on the list. Subsequently, you will have built a pattern of unselfish giving that will be unparalleled to any covetousness for $money or things that might tempt you in the future.

It is said that breaking up is hard to do, and for many adult believers, breaking up the relationship with $money is next to impossible. You can either go at it cold turkey by closing your mind to the possible losses and opening your eyes to the foreseeable gains and trusting God once and for all. I say trusting God once and for all, because when you commit yourself to Him you will see His benevolent hand at work in your life so that you are never without life's necessities from that day forth. The other option is to wait to tithe when a need for God's intervention in your life's affairs comes up. When you are in a crisis. While this is not advisable, I concede that it will give you the opportunity to prove God, and to witness His faithfulness first hand, which will affirm faith and trust within you, if you let Him in wholeheartedly. Or you can simply go on living your presumed Christian way of life in total denial and self deceit, and not see the grand works of God manifested on your behalf. Those who live this way fail to prove God and wind up living their lives in doubt and turmoil.

> For if there be first a willing mind, it is
> accepted according to that a man hath,
> and not according to that he hath not.
>
> *2 Corinthians 8:12*

$Money in Your Relationship

You can sarcastically conclude that the way to avoid conflict when it comes to money is to not lend or give any of your own. This will falsely comfort you into thinking you have solved the $Money problem, but it is only a deception since it does not address the calling in God's Word.

> For, brethren, ye have been called unto
> liberty; only use not liberty for an
> occasion to the flesh, but by love serve

one another. For all the law is fulfilled
in one word, even in this; Thou shalt
love thy neighbour as thyself.

Galatians 5: 13—14

Here is the problem; we are to serve one another by love. If you withhold the world's goods from your brethren in need, how then can you comply with this rule? Does it mean to give your money to others or lend it, regardless of how undeserving they may be? Who, then is to judge when it is the right situation to give or to lend, and when it is not? What does the Word have to say regarding this? Let's look into this a little deeper.

Acts 4:34-35 details how the believers of that day unselfishly sold their excess possessions, brought the proceeds to the Church, and the Church divided among the people according to need. The most impressive thing to see is how the people were moved in their hearts to do the thing that at any other time would have been very arduous to do. They sold their lands and their extra stuff to give the proceeds to the Church willingly (and I might add, lovingly) for the benefit of others who had not even asked them for help, it was all left up to the Church to administer. There is a "big elephant in the room" that seldom gets the proper attention when it comes to tithing, offerings, and plurality giving in the Church. That elephant is that the givers feel compelled to get an accountability for their contribution of how and to whom their money gets used for. This is not consistent with doctrine. You are to give out of your heart, as a cheerful giver, and it is left for the Church to determine how the gifts are applied. Once you've made your contribution, you no longer have a say in the matter. Contemporary charitable giving is tainted with giving for a specific purpose, but such is not the case with the Church. Your giving is not for satisfying a specific church need, but a giving out of love in obedience to the commandment, which once out of your hand relieves you of any further responsibility, but accrues to your blessing. The giving is between you and God, not the Church. Of course, it is common place in today's Churches to do special fund raisers, and while I'm not a fan of this type of coerced giving, I suppose that it's fine if everyone is in accord. However, I would categorize that as abundant giving, and disassociated from the tithing responsibility, which is always a matter of your heart concerning God, and how much you trust Him to do better for you with the 90% you've retained, than you could do with the 100% of your increase. I also believe that fund raisers are laced with concerns of creating personal problems relating to pride, bragging, guilt and shame of the least able believers, and it opens the door for generating preference measured by the amount of the gift. God is not a respecter of persons, and the Lord points this out throughout the Gospel. The Church should pray to God for its needs daily, and trust in God's faithfulness to provide, as did George Muller in London for the needs of the orphanage, and never went without the needs being met. He "dared to believe that God both could and would supply all of his need".

Let's look closer at what happened in chapter four of Acts and explore what took place to cause this marvelous and unsolicited universal turn of events of believers freely giving their surplus to the Church.

We can see from the record that prayer was involved, a very deep and intense prayer that shook the house. Then, the Holy Spirit came upon them, and all of a sudden, people were doing the unthinkable. They sold their surplus lands and possessions to give to the Church to distribute to the poor according to need. You should bear in mind that prior to this inspired motivation, these folks had been greatly moved by events surrounding the miracle performed by Peter and John on the lame man. Not to mention, the turnabout from the usual harsh treatment, punishment, and imprisonment of the saints by the Sanhedrin to an almost passive treatment of Peter and John.

The believers highly exalted God and the Lord Jesus, in whose name they were forbidden to speak by the powers to be in authority at the Temple. The believers got together and prayed. You may be saying to yourself, "Good for them, but what does this have to do with me? What does this have to do with me and my love of $money?"

For them in the book of Acts it was all about seeing the magnificence of God, His hand of providence and His eminent rule over man at work. For you in today's world it's about understanding that God wants you to put Him first, before anything else in your life, and that you show Him that you have truly put Him first by relinquishing your hold and desire for material things, including $money, and relying totally on Him. As you comply with God's command regarding the firstfruits of your increase, you demonstrate that you trust Him to provide for your every need in every situation.

Your relationship with others will be greatly enlarged if you can view it as not dependent on resources, but dependent on God. If you can surrender your fear of being without and together with your friends, spouse, children, employees, and others who play a significant role in your life, start to rely on God to make life's necessary provisions available to you, then you will prosper together beyond measure. God challenges you to come into His presence together in prayer in your relationship, being of one mind and of one accord as to your needs, wants, and desires, and to allow Him to fulfill the desires of your heart. But, should you come divided in purpose or divided in intent, your benefit will be at best a smaller portion of all that has otherwise been set aside for you, if you had come united together as one with a pure heart for God. Do not be inclined to giving to gain popularity, neither become engrossed with concern about how your gifts will be spent.

In marriage you must approach your personal relationship not as two separate sets of finances (his and hers), but as one, just as in marriage you are the one flesh. You are not two households, but one. The details of how to make it work, though complicated, must be worked out by you in the sight of God. You can start by setting time aside and preparing a total and complete disclosure of income and expenses. Prepare a real and comprehensive family budget. Begin to work at this today. Take the initiative. Be the first. Take the lead, be the servant leader the Lord Jesus described. Learn to separate yourself from the love of $money, and unite yourself with your loved one, or if in business, unite yourself with those whom you have chosen to partner with. And most important, partner with God.

Whether in a business partnership or marriage, the relationship must define with clarity each one's role and the percent of each partner's contribution toward accomplishing the goals. The percentage of your contribution should be consistent with, and in relationship to your ability to produce, that is what matters in this case, not the amount contributed. You want to confirm to each other that you're making the adequate and requisite contribution toward achieving the goal, and that you are putting your one hundred percent into the relationship. Carefully review that what each partner is expected to contribute is clear to both regarding the financial goals of the relationship, and that they possess the ability to meet the expectation.

ALWAYS IN REMEMBRANCE: 2 PETER 1:15

1. The _____ of $Money is the root of all evil.
2. The unchecked status of finances may lead to _____ in the relationship.
3. Desire for $Money can _____ us to do strange things.
4. We use $money to _____ our social status.
5. Your relationship with $Money _____ your relationship with others.
6. The tendency to love $Money is a _____ in man.
7. The first _____ of all belongs to God.
8. We are to serve one another by _____ not by the value of our money.
9. Surrender your _____ to God, and allow Him to fulfill the desires of your heart.
10. Approach your relationship not as two _____ finances, but as one.

SCRIPTURE REFERENCE:

1 Timothy 6:10; Leviticus 27:30; 2 Corinthians 8:12; Galatians 5:13-14; Acts 4:34

XIV.

How Much
Forgiveness, Lord?

HIGHER GROUND PRINCIPLE # 20

Have unlimited forgiveness for others as
God has for you.

The problem we encounter with forgiveness is that there is no gray area to dwell in. Forgiveness is absolute and complete. For example, love, according to the Word, is an absolute condition to be fulfilled. Yet, you may choose to love according to how you feel or how you perceive that you have been made to feel. In your own mind, love is measured in varying degrees, depending on how you feel about the person. You reason that you either love someone a little or that you are working on loving them. So, your love is conditional, and worse than that, conditional love is inconsistent from person to person, and is based on conditions that may vary as your emotions move up and down the spectrum.

One way of establishing consistency in loving others is through your willingness to forgive. You may be more willing to forgive one person over another or one trespass over another. Yet, the requirement is to forgive all.

Forgiveness does not afford you the luxury to fantasize about it. It is absolute, just as God's unconditional love for you is absolute. You cannot reason varying degrees of forgiveness in your mind, because it just does not work that way. You may not be able to bring yourself to completely forgive a person because the offense, as you see it, does not compare with your level of pride and sense of fairness regarding the matter. You may feel that the perpetrator is not worthy of being absolved, therefore, forgiveness does not fit into your way of thinking. However, from God's perspective forgiveness is not about the other person. Forgiveness is required of you by God in order to unburden you from carrying extra baggage on your trip through life. You are to have complete and total forgiveness of others, and if you fail to comply with this, you will have fallen short of complying with God's commandment. You cannot change God's commandment in the slightest bit, the change must come from you in how you think and perceive the requirement to forgive. You can't skate around this issue and say you have forgiven a little, or that you are on the road to forgiveness. Maybe you can do enough to look good in the eyes of your friends and those around you, but you're not looking good in the eyes of God. You may be cool with your friends, but you are not cool with the Lord Jesus if you have not forgiven all.

You also have people in your relationship whose behavior is constantly begging for forgiveness. This is the question that plagued Peter, and brought him to seek justification from Jesus, and it is a question most of us rarely dare ask openly, though it needs to be asked frequently within yourself, "How many times am I to forgive someone?". Your position on forgiveness may favor not forgiving, instead of being forgiving. You want to see repentance on the part of the aggressor before you offer up any semblance of your precious generosity to forgive. You want to hear those two words, "I'm sorry." When you finally come around to wanting to fulfill the Christian requirement to forgive, your reluctance to be forgiving might result in a conversation with the Lord similar to the encounter He had with Peter.

The Lord:	You are to forgive.
You:	Lord, I will forgive him this one time, if he promises never to do that again. That's all I'm willing to do.
The Lord:	No. That's not good enough.
You:	Okay, Lord. I'll forgive him seven times.

The Lord:	Ha, ha, ha! Seven times?
You:	All right, Lord. I'll forgive him seven times seven!
The Lord:	No, my child. Try at least seventy times seven. How about if you forgive him 490 times? Then come back and talk to me about it.

Until you have fulfilled the will of the Lord, there is little or nothing you can say to Him or ask of Him with any right of expectation. You may find that you pray often over the situation, and the desired result doesn't come. Why? It doesn't come because you have yet to forgive in your heart.

> Then came Peter to him, and said,
> Lord, how oft shall my brother sin
> against me, and I forgive him? Till
> seven times? Jesus saith unto him, I say
> not unto thee, Until seven times: but,
> Until seventy times seven.

Matthew 18:21—22

In the Kingdom of God, there is no limit placed on forgiveness. Forgiveness is always in style and expected on demand. A checking account is called a demand deposit. This means that the bank must give up the money whenever the owner of the account asks for it, on demand. Forgiveness is a demand account of the Lord's. It is not you who demands forgiveness from the other person; rather, it is the Lord who demands forgiveness of others from you. The reason He can demand this forgiveness is expressed in the following Parable. (Parables — are stories, especially those told by Jesus to provide a vision of life, especially life in God's Kingdom. Parable means a putting alongside for purposes of comparison and new understanding. Parables utilize (word) pictures such as metaphors or similes and frequently extend them into a brief story to make a point or disclosure. Holman, Bible Dictionary, p. 1071).

Therefore is the kingdom of heaven
likened unto a certain king, which
would take account of his servants. And
when he had begun to reckon, one was
brought unto him, which owed him ten
thousand talents.

Matthew 18:23—33

Ten thousand is a very large sum in any currency. It should cause you to want to explore the context of such a large number. Also, what is a talent? Surely this is not referring to "American Idol" on television. Whatever a talent is, this servant owed his master 10,000 of them.

A talent is a measure of about 75 pounds, as we would understand it today. One talent is worth about 750 ounces of silver. A talent has also been defined as a measure equivalent to more than fifteen years labor for one worker. This guy owed 10,000 talents. It would take 150,000 years of labor or 7,500,000 ounces of silver to pay it back. That's a total of 468,750 pounds of silver or 1,000 laborers working for fifteen years. The debt was enormous, and it was unlikely that the servant would be able to pay it off.

But forasmuch as he had not to pay,
his lord commanded him to be sold,
and his wife, and children, and all
that he had, and payment to be made.
The servant therefore fell down, and
worshipped him, saying, Lord, have
patience with me, and I will pay thee
all. Then the lord of that servant was
moved with compassion, and loosed
him, and *forgave him the debt.*

...But the same servant went out, and
found one of his fellow servants, which
owed him an hundred pence...

100 pence is worth 1/8th of an ounce of silver or about one day's wages. How could this possibly compare to 150,000 years of labor? The comparison is around 54.8 million to one.

> ...and he laid hands on him, and took
> him by the throat, saying, Pay me that
> thou owest. And his fellow servant fell
> down at his feet, and besought him,
> saying, Have patience with me, and I
> will pay thee all. And he would not: but
> went and cast him into prison, till he
> should pay the debt.

How awful for this servant not to have learned the lesson of forgiveness taught him by his master, and followed his master's example of forgiveness. Wouldn't the master have been proud of his servant and gratified that he had done the right thing for his servant? Wouldn't he have been happy that his example was well received and that it might have started a virtuous cycle among his servants, his household, his neighborhood, and throughout the land? What a terrible missed opportunity by this greedy and selfish servant to please his master and to bless his fellow man.

> So when his fellowservants saw what was
> done, they were very sorry, and came
> and told unto their lord all that was
> done. Then his lord, after that he had
> called him, said unto him, O *thou wicked*
> *servant*, I forgave thee all that debt,
> because thou desiredst me: *Shouldest*
> *not thou also have had compassion on thy*
> *fellowservant, even as I had pity on thee?*

When you fail to forgive you are nothing less than a wicked servant. Can you see now why so few of us, if any, are ever worthy to receive anything from the Lord? He has given you a rich benefit in that you do not have to pay the penalty of sin. You have been pardoned completely. Jesus is not charging you for the forgiveness you have received. Jesus made payment for you by the sacrifice of His innocent life for you, when you were the least worthy of being forgiven. You owe it to the Lord to forgive others as He forgave you. The trespasses of others against you do not compare with your trespass against God.

What you must take away from this parable is that you have better forgive others. It is in your best interest to forgive if you want to be accounted as an obedient believer and follower of the Lord. Not forgiving puts you in defiance of the Lord's commandment.

> And his lord was wroth, and delivered
> him to the tormentors, till he should pay
> all that was due unto him. So likewise
> shall my heavenly Father do also unto
> you, if ye from your hearts forgive not
> every one his brother their trespasses.
>
> *Matthew 18:34—35*

Reality can be very harsh. Verse 35 leaves no wiggle room. It says "likewise shall My Heavenly Father do also unto you." This is a promise with the power and authority for being fulfilled. You will be delivered to the tormentors for failure to forgive. You have been forgiven for so much, yet you find it so difficult to forgive someone else. Carefully consider the consequences, and acknowledge that failure to forgive is a sin.

> Whoso stoppeth his ears at the cry of
> the poor, he also shall cry himself, but
> shall not be heard.
>
> *Proverbs 21:13*

And forgive us our debts, as we forgive
our debtors.

Matthew 6: 12

For he shall have judgment without
mercy, that hath shewed no mercy; and
mercy rejoiceth against judgment.

James 2:13

It is remarkable how forgiveness is designed to operate in your life. If you are unforgiving, then you are unnecessarily laden with a heavy burden. You can remove this burden by your own free will desire to do so. If you are laden down with too may burdens, you will become sluggish, tired, and unable to move. This is a spiritual law, and the consequences are manifested in your spiritual life. Perhaps you are that one person that really loves God and wants so much to do His will. You want to have fellowship with likeminded believers and be a significant part of the household, but you encounter every difficulty and barrier in getting to church; waking on time for fellowship meetings, having to overcome obstacles in order to get to prayer night, and so on. If you should be the one having these kinds of experiences, you might want to consider that it may be a spiritual matter that needs to be dealt with. It might just be that you are too overloaded with sin and guilt and overwhelmed by the weight of your unforgiving heart. Let it go. Let go and let God do what is best for you. Forgive.

Let the Word of God speak to your heart. If you want to have good and meaningful godly relationships, your heart must be prepared to partake with them. If you are not weighted down, then you will be able to freely enjoy your relationship with God and with Jesus.

Cast thy burden upon the LORD, and
he shall sustain thee: he shall never
suffer the righteous to be moved.

Psalm 55:22

ALWAYS IN REMEMBRANCE: 2 PETER 1:15

1. There is no _____ area to dwell in when it comes to forgiveness.
2. We are often _____ to forgive others.
3. The Lord _____ that you forgive others.
4. Forgiveness may start a _____ cycle in your relationship.
5. Not forgiving _____ you down with heavy burdens.
6. You can freely _____ your relationship if your heart is not weighted down.

SCRIPTURE REFERENCE:

Matthew 18:21—22; Matthew 18:23—33; Matthew 18:34—35;

Proverbs 21:13; Matthew 6:12; James 2:13; Psalms 55:22

XV.

A Soft Answer Turns Away Wrath *and* Iron Does Sharpen Iron

HIGHER GROUND PRINCIPLE #21

Measure your words and avoid offending others.

There are two biblical principles to uphold that will affect your relationship positively, or conversely, if ignored will allow negativity to set in. If you err in these two marvelous biblical principles, your misunderstanding will have an adverse affect on your relationship. When properly applied, however, these are two powerful principles to live by and from which to harvest fruit in the relationship for a long time. They are spiritual laws that work seamlessly in your relationship to accomplish their purpose.

> A soft answer turneth away wrath: but
> grievous words stir up anger.

Proverbs 15:1

Why should you give a soft answer? This principle has one purpose and that is to quench fiery buildup in an argument. Simply put, lower your tone, respond with a kind word, and keep from shooting out darts of retort that infuriate the other person; it lowers the temperature of emotions. The effect will be to quiet down the situation until cooler heads prevail and you have a better climate for handling the details of the issue. The purpose in applying this principle is never to teach the other person a lesson or to improve upon their social skills, but solely to bring peace.

The concept of iron sharpening iron

Iron sharpeneth iron; so a man
sharpeneth the countenance of his friend.

Proverbs 27: 17

On the other hand, iron does sharpen iron. I have the distinguished job of sharpening the knives in the kitchen. This is a job that I perform, whenever I can get around to it, but I always do a poor job of it. One of my daughters is quick to criticize. She can't understand why our knives are always dull. My desired response to her comment is to say, "Maybe it's because they get used often to prepare meals. Something you should try doing someday." However, that would not be a soft answer. That would be a harsh and provoking answer, and the Word says we should not provoke our children to wrath. I think that includes our adult children, as well.

For the knives in the kitchen to get sharpened, they must be rubbed on a file, flint, metal or stone to sharpen them. If rubbed against a sponge, there would be gentle contact, which would not result in sharpening the knife. And so it is in our lives, as well. Sometimes the Word of God will hit you like an anvil dropping on a foot. At first it hurts, and it pains you to listen, to accept it, and to obey it. It rarely fails in a marriage counseling session that when the wife is told what the Word says about submitting to her husband that the hackles go up. When angry or disappointed, wives hear what the Word in Ephesians 5:22, that wives are to submit, but they reject it. They say, "Oh, no. I'm not going to submit to him!" By her accounting there are many reasons not to submit to her husband. But the Word is still true and to be obeyed.

Right about now, husbands are usually grinning from cheek to cheek, until I read further in verse 25 where it says that husbands are to love their wives as Jesus Christ loves the church. That definitely brings the husband down, from grin heaven down to earth. Their response is, "Oh, no! I don't have to love her if she is mean to me or if she doesn't give me love and respect!". What he is trying to say is, "I don't have to love her if she is not fulfilling my desires." His basis for loving his wife is conditional, the opposite of God's love which is unconditional.

In either case, the Word is like iron. If the recipient of the Word were made of iron, he or she would allow the Word to rub into him or her until they got sharp. To be sharpened by the Word is to receive it with meekness and humility and being convicted in the heart with desire to obey it. Realizing that it is God speaking to you through His Word and that you will obey Him and accept to apply His hand to resolve all conflict regarding the matter. The fact is that when either or both spouses apply these principles without constraint, the result will be remarkable. The marital relationship will soon turn into a positive one. When rubbed against, the iron in the Word it sharpens the iron in the man in a positive and constructive way, and the heart of the man is prepared to obey and to do the will of God. The man receives a sharp edge to be able to discern, to slice through, between the values imposed by worldly living and those found in godly living. (Hebrews 4:12). Regardless the complexity or overwhelming difficulty, the matter will be resolved with the least pain inflicted on either party. Both parties will be able to lovingly apply the concept of FRB, doing what is fair to each, what is right by each, and what is best for the relationship.

God uses the iron of His ways to chastise men and women of God and to sharpen them up so that they come to their godly senses. The prodigal son sharpened up only after he had spent all his inheritance and felt compelled to take slop from the pigs to feed his hunger. Only then did he realize how much was provided for the lowliest servant in his father's house and how the abundance of food was of much better quality than pig slop. The chastening sharpened him up and gave him vision to see through the evil choices he had made, and gave him the courage to return to face his father in the hope of being received to the lowliest position of servant in his father's household.

And the younger of them said to his father, Father, give me the portion of goods that falleth to me. And he divided unto them his living. And not many days after the younger son gathered all together, and took his journey into a far country, and there wasted his substance with riotous living. And when he had spent all, there arose a mighty famine in that land; and he began to be in want. And he went and joined himself to a citizen of that country; and he sent him into his fields to feed swine. And he would fain have filled his belly with the husks that the swine did eat: and no man gave unto him. And when he came to himself, he said, How many hired servants of my father's have bread enough and to spare, and I perish with hunger! I will arise and go to my father, and will say unto him, Father, I have sinned against heaven, and before thee.

Luke 15: 12—18

Neither hypocrisy nor harshness makes you sharp:

Some people are always trying to be politically correct in every situation. They try hard not to offend anyone. They never say anything that can be mistaken for criticism by another, nor do they confront their friends, even when it is warranted. These are kind persons who don't want to hurt other people's feelings, or they may be persons who desire to remain agreeable to others so that they are liked and thought of in a positive light. This is hypocrisy, and it should never be tolerated, especially in a relationship. A relationship requires that each person is honest and truthful without resorting to words or tactics that are insulting, hurtful, or harsh toward their partner. Some may grasp at the opportunity in a disagreement to unload things they have had on their chests under the guise of positive criticism, but that is not acceptable either, because it is insincere and lacks in integrity. So, the sharpening of iron in the person requires truth and honesty in place of hypocrisy, and integrity and sincerity in the place of a guise for dumping on your partner. A healthy relationship is built on THIS, saying the truth, being honest, responding from integrity, and sincerely desiring only for the best outcome for all involved and the perseverance of the relationship.

A healthy relationship should not be expected to be a bed of roses all the time. Being truthful, honest, and sincere can cause friction and give off some friendly sparks from time to time. If handled properly, constructive criticism is exactly the type of iron sharpening iron that is needed, the sharpening of each other's countenance in the relationship. When both partners in the relationship are walking and living by the Word, each becomes a useful tool made of iron with which to sharpen the other. The end result of controlled and well-placed abrasion brings improvement in the quality of the persons in the relationship. It sharpens up and improves the quality of the relationship. Jesus, it can be said, roughed Peter up several times. One time, He told Peter to get behind Him, Satan. (Matthew 16:23). At another time, as He lifted Peter from sinking in the water, He told Peter he was of little faith. (Matthew 14:31). These were strong words, but they sharpened the rough edges of the fisherman who became a fisher of men. After the Lord's ascension Peter rose up and assumed spiritual leadership for the trembling disciples who previously were locked up in an upper room for fear of what the leaders of the Jews and the local authorities might do to them. Peter's boldness and leadership in the Gospel can be seen throughout the book of Acts and the following epistles, including the Epistles he authored (Acts 2:14—40).

ALWAYS IN REMEMBRANCE: 2 PETER 1:15

1. A soft answer to an angered partner is for the purpose of bringing about _____.
2. It is not necessary to have hard and _____ responses in your conversation.
3. Accepting the _____ in God's Word can be very confronting.
4. God's unbending ways are like iron to _____ and sharpen a man.
5. Sharpening from God is to bring us back to our _____.
6. _____ in a relationship should not be tolerated.
7. A relationship can have _____ but constructive confrontation.
8. Well placed constructive _____ improves the quality of a relationship.

SCRIPTURE REFERENCE:

Proverbs 15:1; Proverbs 27:17; Ephesians 5:22, 25; Matthew 16:23; Matthew 14:31;

Acts 2:14-40; Hebrews 4:12; Luke 15:12-18

XVI.

THE PERFECT PARTNERSHIP

HIGHER GROUND PRINCIPLE # 22

Form a perfect partnership in your relationship as did Jesus with God, and as Jesus desires to have with you.

The culmination of a healthy relationship is the perfect partnership. On earth, this is a rare sighting, if actually ever seen. We have more examples of poor and dysfunctional partnerships than perfect partnerships. There is only one place to turn for a respite from what we see all around us. The relationship between God and Jesus provides the keys to unlocking the secrets of the perfect relationship. This is what Building Blocks for Relationships has attempted to describe. Building blocks are fundamental in children's learning. They teach that you can firmly support a third block by placing it atop two other blocks laid side by side. Applying this concept enlarges the understanding for constructing a building with sound footings, solid foundations and weight bearing walls rising to support the roof. These elements for building a house serve the same purpose as truth, honesty, integrity and sincerity (THIS), as the foundational blocks for building a relationship. The relationship must be constructed on top of a foundation built on solid ground for optimum strength and support.

God loves Jesus, and Jesus loves God. They have clarity with regards to who is in charge and who is the ultimate decision maker; there is no doubt between them. However, despite His prevailing authority, God will not violate Jesus' free will to exercise His own will should Jesus choose to exercise free will. God would respect Him for any choice Jesus would make.

> And he said, Abba, Father, all things are
> possible unto thee; take away this cup
> from me: nevertheless not what I will,
> but what thou wilt.

Mark 14:36

Relying on the experience of His perfect relationship with His Father, Jesus asks that we take His yoke upon us and learn from Him. Everyone can profit by sticking close to Jesus and learning how to build relationships. In simple English, He would say, "Partner up with me. I know the ins and outs of how to have and maintain a perfect relationship. Let's model a partnership after the example of My Father and Me." Consider the words spoken in the following scripture.

> All things are delivered unto me of my
> Father: and no man knoweth the Son,
> but the Father; neither knoweth any
> man the Father, save the Son, and he to
> whomsoever the Son will reveal him.
> Come unto me, all ye that labour and are
> heavy laden, and I will give you rest. Take
> my yoke upon you, and learn of me; for I
> am meek and lowly in heart: and ye shall
> find rest unto your souls. For my yoke is
> easy, and my burden is light.

Matthew 11:27-30.

Jesus describes the intimacy of His relationship with God. He says that no man knows either Him or Me the way that He knows Me and the way that I know Him. We have something special. We have a healthy and robust relationship. We have the perfect partnership. Jesus appeals to our understanding, in a sense, by coaxing us into wanting to partner with Him. Who among us does not labor day after day, sometimes over the same thing? We are heavy laden, weighted down with the issues of life, with our emotional battles, a heavy load of guilt and shame weighing us down, refusing to be forgiving, and trying to exist with our crippled relationships. All of mankind is in need of rest. Jesus promises rest to all who labor and are weighted down, if they will come to Him.

Let us suppose that a very wealthy person knocked on your door one day and said, "Here is a contract, a partnership agreement. I promise to put up all the money that you will ever need to do business with me. Moreover, you don't have to do much of the work. I will take care of that for us. What I want you to do is just keep me company, be loyal, and do what I ask of you. I promise not to abuse our relationship or ask you to do any wrong. "What would you say? You would say, "Yes, yes, yes. My ship finally came in. I'm finally getting the break I deserve." You would throw your shoulders back and be proud of yourself. You would stumble and fall running for a pen to sign the partnership agreement.

Jesus's offer is for you to partner with Him. If you become His partner He will take the load off your back and give you the light chores to do. He will relieve you of the hardships of life and replace them with joy and prosperity. Once you partner with Jesus, you will transform and become like Him. It is at this point in your spiritual maturity that you will be able to extend yourself to others and build a relationship that is modeled after your relationship with the Lord. Your relationships on earth will include Him. You will form that three string cord which is not easily broken (Ecclesiastes 4: 12b).

You will dwell in THIS: truth, honesty, integrity, and sincerity. You will weave the concepts of sanctification, sacrifice, substitution, submission, and survival of your relationship into your very fiber of life. You will be the driving force to work spiritual laws into your relationship, and the results will propel your relationship into a perfect partnership where soft words are spoken to take away wrath and where constructive criticism works to sharpen the partners and improve the quality of the relationship. You will become the catalyst for forming the perfect partnership relationship on earth with everyone you choose to partner with.

ALWAYS IN REMEMBRANCE: 2 PETER 1:15

1. A _____ relationship is the ultimate in making the perfect partnership.
2. Jesus has the _____ partnership with God.
3. By developing a relationship with Jesus, you construct a _____ for relationships on earth.
4. A perfect partnership enjoys intimacy and _____ in its core.
5. Partnership with Jesus brings _____ and prosperity into your life.
6. Spiritual maturity allows you to _____ your relationship with God into your relationship with others.

SCRIPTURE REFERENCE:

Mark 14:36; Matthew 11:27—30: Ecclesiastes 4:12

XVII.

A RELATIONSHIP *with* GOD *the* FATHER

A relationship which is true and pure can be best described as an equation. A relationship exists in perfect balance when it has THIS on both sides of the equal sign, intact. The attributes found in THIS are absolute. That is, each attribute exists in the quantity of 100%, and anything less is no longer the attribute. For example, a half-truth is no longer the truth, nor is a partial truth even if it's mostly true. Also, being 90% honest means that you are not an honest person, honesty exists as 100%. Likewise, acting insincere from time to time means that you lack sincerity, and going back on your word once puts cracks in your wall of integrity. The cracks are the beginning of the breaches that are bound to form in your wall of integrity, and if there are cracks, it is no longer whole and intact. It lacks integrity, just as you will lack integrity when you lie or cheat in your relationship.

A breakdown in the relationship does not mean that the relationship has come to its end. It can be fixed, as was God's relationship with man after the betrayal by Adam. God provided a road back to the balance in the relationship through forgiveness. Man accepts forgiveness offered by God through repentance, and this also is the first step on the road to repair a broken relationship. There are two problems that prevent repentance. One is man's ignorance to avail himself of forgiveness, and the second is man's unwillingness to repent. On the one hand, not knowing that you can be forgiven is an awful handicap to preserving the relationship with God, and so many have turned away from God by seeking absolution from other gods, or choosing to exist in self-denial, thinking that they don't need God. Others grasp at repentance, but want it on their own terms, or want only the part that suits their egos, ignores their guilt, and allows self-denial to prevail. The simple truth is that God wants you to renew your mind and to change your heart from lust, covetousness, etc., to a pure heart, as did David when he asked of God in Psalm 91:10, when he realized that he couldn't do it by himself and needed God's help.

In the relationship equation with God all things are in balance. We have the example of Jesus and the Father to go by. They were and continue in perfect balance because the same parts exist on both sides of the equation. For man, the equation falls out of balance because we cannot uphold all of the components on our side of the equation. Through temptation, our culture and the selfish desires of men, we cannot always help to avoid sin. Sin is the destroyer of the relationship between God and man, but God built in a process for restoring balance to the relationship when it falters. God put in place forgiveness of sin, and made full payment with the life of His Son so that men can return to the balance in the relationship equation when they repent.

The Relationship Equation

T.H.I.S.		T.H.I.S.
FORGIVENESS	**=**	**REPENTANCE**
by		by
GOD		**MAN**

God loved man first. It was due to His love that God sought to have a relationship with man, and to create a family based on righteous principles of love. Our proper response is to love God in return, even if there were no notable benefits, our first response should be to return the love we have been given. We can demonstrate our love for God by abiding by His requests. They can be understood as rules, commandments, precepts, laws, etc., but they are what God requests of us, and it should be accepted as His command. In addition, because we are His creation we should only seek to praise and worship Him as our creator, and out of thankfulness for all He does to be the sufficiency for all of our needs and all of our righteous wants. Yahweh's sovereign lordship is worthy of all that we have to give in obedience to His precepts and our praise and worship of Him.

Imagine, if you could fathom the complexity of the human body. Each cell has a specific function and purpose. The individual organs comprised of cells form a complex system in conjunction with specific fluids, hormones, enzymes and so much more. Then all the systems articulate together to form what we experience as our body. This is not a biology session, but rather a reflection on how complicated our bodies are. The creator took everything necessary into consideration when He formed, made and created man. Another thought to take in is the DNA and RNA which hold and convey the unique architecture and engineering specifications for each individual human being. We are given a glimpse into spiritual aspects of Angels and other spiritual beings. Now try to imagine how complex "spirit" must be, given how spiritual beings are described and their actions. God created the spiritual beings. God is not described in the same way, although that's the perceived identity we conjure up when we think of Him. God is the eternal being. The substance of His makeup transcends far beyond what any human can describe or understand.

That is the most important aspect for us to understand about this incredible eternal being who possesses the power and authority to create spirit, to create the material universe in what we know so far to be of an infinite magnitude, and yet, He, our God, Yahweh, wants to have a personal relationship with me, and with you, and with all humans. The thought boggles the mind farther than anything I can process. Having the privilege of the opportunity to establish communication with such an awesome being makes my head spin. Why wouldn't I want that, especially when He is offering nothing but good in a relationship with Him. That I can have a relationship with God boggles the mind, but that He offers me to be in His family and to be with Him for eternity, now that's something I can't refuse. I want to have the best relationship with the Father and with His son, as I can possibly have. Don't you want to wrap both arms around this opportunity and never let go?

There are certain precepts that God has set in place by which we confirm our relationship with Him. They consist of the most fundamental observances on our part, that must be complied with to maintain fellowship with Almighty God, and to receive eternal salvation at the end times. These precepts are very succinct and are spelled out throughout the Scriptures. They go beyond observance of the ten commandments and the precepts for relationships with other men. They speak to the things that God holds man in the highest personal accountability for, because God, Himself holds these up to the highest value in His relationship with man, which is why you need to be knowledgeable of them, and assure that you comply with them at all times.

The Law contains many admonishments which must all be complied with in order to fulfill the Law. The Lord Jesus provided the Christian with a very succinct guide to fulfilling all the Law; to love God with all your heart, soul, and mind, and to love your neighbor as yourself. The admonishments listed below transcend beyond the Lord's command by drilling down into specific dos and don'ts that God totally frowns upon when they are violated. They deal with stumbling blocks that if not overcome will remain barriers for entry into the Kingdom of God. If you are living out the great commandment you will most likely not have to be concerned about violating these admonishments, but otherwise, it is good for you to heed their warnings.

1. There shall be no other god before YAHWEH. (Exodus 20:3)
2. You shall not take the name of the LORD your God in vain. (Exodus 20:7)
3. You are to love God with all your heart, soul and mind. (Matthew 22:37-38)
4. You must honor the Son (John 5:23)
5. Jesus is the only way to the Father (John 14:6)
6. You are to love your neighbor, as you love yourself. (Matthew 22:39)
7. The just shall live by faith. (Hebrews 10:38)
8. Never Blaspheme against the Holy Spirit (Mark 3:29
9. Don't grieve the Holy Spirit (Ephesians 4:30)
10. Strive for peace with everyone, and for holiness without which no one will see the Lord (Hebrews 12:14)

God's one great desire is for you to enter into His Kingdom and to be with Him and the Lord Jesus for ever more. All the work to get you into the Kingdom has been done by the Father, and the remaining works were completed by the Lord Jesus Christ. There remains a portion of the effort which requires your commitment and labor to perform and uphold your part. You, however are responsible to hold up your end by living a holy life, and showing God moment by moment that you hold His precepts in the highest regard; that they hold the highest position of authority over you. God wants you to be part of His eternal family, and it is up to you to want to be in it, to the end that you sacrifice your wants, lusts and desires in this life, so you can partake of the eternal joy which is to come.

XVIII.

A LASTING FINISH

I have titled this study Building Blocks for Relationships. It is intended as a guide that gently imparts the godly purposes you should have in your relationship. This book is designed to offer you the opportunity to change how you perceive and approach your relationships with others. Every relationship can afford to change in some way for its improvement.

Among the objectives, is to make you aware of the rudiments that comprise a godly relationship in the hope that you elect to adopt the Christian biblical principles that will affect positive change in your relationships now and throughout your life. This is a guide book to spiritual laws that work the same all the time, and work the same for everyone, if the prescribed conditions are met. In that sense, it is a rulebook that applies in every case and will guide you back to God and His Word regarding how to relate to others. A successful relationship will exist when two people adhere to and apply Christian principles. A healthy solution may be had even if at first only one person is willing to apply the principles and live by godly standards. My desire is that you continue in prayer and trust in our Lord Jesus Christ, the Messiah, and through Him, fortify your understanding of how to go about improving your relationship through godliness. I hope that you will use this study as a building block in your quest and pursuit for a relationship at a higher spiritual and godly place in your life.

An example of a pure and perfect relationship is provided in God, the Father, and His son, Jesus. What is absent from their relationship is that neither one tried to negatively influence, lie to, or deceive the other on something they did not intend to do in order to leverage control over the other; a thing so prevalent in human interactions. They could have elected to hypocritically handle their interrelationship without truth, honesty, integrity, or sincerity (THIS) in their intentions or communication. This is far from being the case. As a matter of fact, we have no better example of a relationship than that of God and Jesus. Like Jesus, we should also endeavor to build our personal relationship with God based on THIS. Our relationship with Jesus is to be established on the same principles as is our relationship with God. In Jesus, we have one more requirement to live up to, and that is to obey His Commandments as were given to Him by the Father. Both God and Jesus have already proven their integrity. It is up to you to prove your integrity in response to establishing a relationship with them. When you have perfected your integrity with God, you will be able to experience similar joy in earthly relationships you establish through the application of the teachings found in the Word. Experience THIS with people and it will prepare you to experience THIS with God. How you relate to others around you, people that you see and touch, is the true measure of how you relate to God, whom you can't see or touch.

The godly relationship begins by the Lord relieving you of your heavy burdens, the things that weigh you down in life, which He takes on as His own burdens in place of you. This occurs when you accept His yoke (when you commit to hitching up with Him), then His promise of rest unto your soul will be realized. By giving your burdens of life over to Him, you are set free from the weighty matters in your life, and you place those weighty matters on Him, as you apply His principles in your life. (Please consult your pastor for further details and assistance on how to make this transition in your spiritual relationship with the Lord. I am certain your pastor will be blessed and eager to help.)

The starting point for improving your earthly relationships or for starting up a new relationship is in the application of truth, honesty, integrity, and sincerity (THIS). Once you have begun a life pattern of basing your relationships on THIS, you will find applying the 5SS' (sanctification—a setting apart; sacrifice—giving up your preference; substitution—putting yourself in their place; submission—giving in to another's point of view; and survival— persevering in the relationship) simpler and easier to do. Doing this will take you to that higher ground.

The Higher Ground Principles are summarized in the Appendix to provide a quick reference, step by step spiritual concepts to apply in the areas of your relationship that need attention, but you will profit most from working every one of them to the fullest of your understanding.

As you open your heart to God and the spiritual principles for relationships, you will also open your heart to your friends. When your relationship with God and the Lord are working well, your relationships with others will work well also. This will bring peace and rest into your life. Ponder these thoughts in light of the following words:

> Come unto me, all ye that labour and
> are heavy laden, and I will give you
> rest. Take my yoke upon you, and
> learn of me; for I am meek and lowly
> in heart: and ye shall find rest unto
> your souls. For my yoke is easy, and my
> burden is light.

Matthew 11:28-30

SUMMARY

Writing a second edition to Building Blocks for Relationships was necessary to expand on several ideas that were presented in the first edition. The first edition offered insight into the spiritual aspects that are not visible to the natural mind. We exist in a natural world and our exposure is to natural things through the five senses. The opinions, theories, theologies and ideas created by men are all that we have to rely upon in the natural realm. Additionally, we are born with a natural mind which comes prepackaged with enmity (an enemy of) God and godly things, right out of the box.

Only through Christ are we given a glimpse to a bigger and broader universe that exists all around us in the spiritual realm. It transcends way beyond what one experiences through the five senses. In Christ we see the transfer of God's mighty power over the natural world made available to men. In the Old Testament Mosses, through God's power, stopped the waters of the Red Sea, made water come out of a rock, and perform other miracles. The prophets likewise, blinded the eyes of the Syrian army, stopped the rain for three years, and summoned fire from Heaven, among other miracles. Every man wants to exercise supernatural power, as was given to a select few in the Old Testament. The great awakening comes to each person individually when they accept Christ as their Lord and begin to witness personal miracles in their lives. The limited power given in olden days to a few individuals is now, through Christ made available to all who accept His Lordship. God in Christ and Christ in you.

There exists a greater spiritual reality that you become connected to when you establish a relationship with Christ, and you put godly principles to work in your life. It opens a window to the spiritual realm of miracles and wonders accessed supernaturally in Christ. In the first edition we introduced the concept of laws. Spiritual laws being immutable and unchanging, and yielding the same result when its conditions are met. That is why we want to employ the precepts taught by the Lord, because they are spiritual laws that you can implement for yourself. Truth, Honesty, Integrity and Sincerity (THIS) are works you can perform in the natural realm while observing godly principles in the spiritual realm. Although you may not see them at work, the fruit that they bear will be the evidence you need to trust that they work.

Observing the Five SS' as you build up your relationship will have the same profitable benefit to your relationship, as will living by the Ten Points of Light, being the Peacemaker, The Salt of the earth, and boldly displaying the Light in you to the world. These are abstract concepts to the human mind, but, since they are spiritual elements, when you apply them, the consistency in their results will prove them out.

In the second edition we introduced the concept of FRB, acting with Fairness, doing the Right thing even if it hurts, and always doing what is Best. When these concepts abide in your heart, your behavior will be positive, resulting in a win/win for all concerned.

A very important Chapter was added titled "A Relationship With God the Father". We regard this an essential part of the relationship complex because it has a two-fold purpose. Having a relationship with the Father requires humility and meekness, as well as all the other precepts presented in the book. It prepares the heart to be acceptable to God, and in so doing, it prepares the heart for having real relationships with fellow men because you would have learned how to apply THIS in the relationship before you establish it. Your relationship with God will be solidified, in that as you treat others in your daily life, you will also tend to treat God the same way. As you become more aware of your earthly, negative behavior, you will be able to renew your mind by looking ahead and changing your behavior to a godly one. A relationship with God is most essential to achieve the higher quality of life on earth, and to serve as the model for your relationships with others.

In the second edition we present ways to differentiate between the natural mind set of your behavior in contrast to the spiritual mind set for a renewed lifestyle of behavior to totally transform you into a man or woman of God. Through this transformation you will be able to better enjoy your partners and associates in relationships. Your life will be enriched and you will experience the closeness that one longs for in every relationship. I pray that you will enjoy reading this edition even more than you did the first edition.

Appendix

ANSWER KEY

ALWAYS IN REMEMBRANCE: (2 PETER 1:15)

Section I
Have THIS...

AIR

1. dealings
2. control
3. THIS
4. correct
5. work, truth
6. faith
7. spiritual
8. lying
9. judge
10. joy

Section II
What Constitutes...

AIR

1. others
2. purpose
3. consider
4. reason
5. clean
6. THIS
7. gain
8. now
9. failure
10. mutual

Section III
The 5 SS'

AIR

1. Sanctification
2. support
3. Sacrifice
4. substitution
5. Submission
6. survival

Section IV
Working to Build...

AIR

1. build
2. will
3. common
4. honor
5. conflict
6. poor
7. respect
8. right

Section V
Examining Faults...

AIR

1. decline
2. vicious
3. unwilling
4. listening
5. diffuse
6. emotional
7. guarded
8. built-up
9. together
10. sacrifices

Section VI
Building Success...

AIR

1. virtuous
2. positive
3. mind
4. emotions
5. nourish
6. decisions
7. repair
8. value

Section VII
Applying Word...

AIR

1. lording
2. commands
3. serve
4. give
5. Sacrificing
6. best
7. leader

Section VIII
Qualities for Christian...

AIR

1. responsibility
2. Accepting
3. teach
4. calling
5. behavior
6. values
7. code
8. offend

Section IX
Offenses Committed...

AIR

1. peacemaker
2. pressure
3. Enduring
4. blessed
5. children
6. preserver
7. equipped
8. calm
9. affect

The Salt of the Earth

AIR

1. peacemakers
2. salt
3. flavoring
4. good
5. lives
6. share

The Light of the World

AIR

1. illuminate
2. daily
3. lead
4. light
5. hidden
6. God

Ten Points of Light

AIR

1. honest
2. good
3. Obey
4. expectation
5. use

6. first
7. disrespect
8. love
9. Hold
10. Honor

Section X
Handling Those Who...

AIR

1. redeemed
2. right
3. reconciled
4. agree
5. straighten
6. avoid

Section XI
Handling Quarrels...

AIR

1. grieves
2. provokes
3. bullying
4. accusation
5. injurious
6. annoying

AIR

1. attitude
2. simmer
3. defensive
4. control
5. Jesus
6. soft

Section XII
The Witness of the Church

AIR

1. peacemakers
2. captives
3. thinking
4. hindered
5. acceptable
6. love
7. discussing
8. resolve
9. witnesses
10. purity

AIR

1. dropped
2. jeopardy
3. impartially
4. reason
5. division
6. bring
7. apply
8. pray

Section XIII
Constraints for Relationships

AIR

1. love
2. ruin
3. compel
4. validate
5. affects
6. fault
7. tenth
8. love
9. fears
10. separate

Section XIV
How Much Forgiveness...

AIR

1. grey
2. reluctant
3. demands
4. virtuous
5. weighs
6. enjoy

Section XV
A Soft Answer...

AIR

1. peace
2. provoking
3. truth
4. chastise
5. senses
6. Hypocrisy
7. friendly
8. criticism

Section XVI
The Perfect Partnership

AIR

1. healthy
2. perfect
3. model
4. loyalty
5. joy
6. extend

HIGHER GROUND (PRINCIPLES)

1. Establish relationships on the principles taught in the Bible
2. Have honest behavior and integrity, and be sincere in everything you do
3. Identify the biblical qualities you want in your relationship
4. Work your relationship for success
5. Apply biblical principles in your relationship
6. Minimize the potential for failure in your relationship
7. Build a virtuous cycle in your relationship through hard work
8. Assert your right to leadership through sacrifice and service
9. Live and walk by the higher and greater standard worthy of the Christian name.
10. Be a peacemaker who brings calm to your relationship
11. Keep the salt flavor for God's Word in you from diluting by temptation and sin
12. Illuminate darkened hearts, help bear another's heavy load, and bring cheer to the sad
13. Let God's light into your heart by relating positively with others
14. Follow the example of forgiveness given by Jesus
15. Avoid quarrels; do not trespass against others
16. Maintain peace, love, and joy in the Church and in your relationship
17. Be a winner in every situation
18. Find a qualified Christian to help resolve a matter
19. Lord, free me from the love of $money and chain my heart to loving you and to loving my brother.
20. Have unlimited forgiveness for others as God has for you.
21. Measure your words and avoid offending others
22. Form a perfect partnership in your relationship as did Jesus with God, and as Jesus desires to have with you.

Workshop Exercises

The workshop exercises will lead you further to having an experience in your relationship reflective of the relationship between God and Jesus. By directly applying scripture to each partner's behavior, you will be establishing healthy expectations of one another, and be encouraged to do what is best for the relationship. The concepts of THIS, FRB, and the 5SS' are encompassed within scripture, and as you apply them you will be achieving the ultimate spiritual fulfillment for you and your loved ones.

THERE ARE SEVEN WORKSHOP EXERCISES. EACH ONE IS DESIGNED FOR A SPECIFIC USER:

1. Woman/Wife
2. Employee
3. Employer
4. Child
5. Parent
6. Friend
7. Man/Husband

The exercises are designed for either group or individual use. The group exercise can be conducted at a meeting of a particular user group (i.e.: women's or men's group) or in a breakout session for a larger diversified group (i.e.: a mixed church group). A round table discussion can be had after group participants have worked individually on their own worksheets, which may prove useful and encouraging to them, and later in a group discussion under the supervision of the group leader. The exercise can also be conducted by a couple at home to assist each other in learning more about biblical responsibilities, and to assist in finding ways for meeting their biblical obligations.

The exercises are designed with selected scriptures germane for each group, where the biblical principles and Christian qualities are defined for each user group. The exercises ask that you read the scripture, review the biblical qualities it addresses, and annotate how you are applying it in your relationship. If it's a quality you are not presently applying, then you are to describe the action you are willing to take to begin applying the said quality. You are encouraged to search the Bible for additional scriptures which you may want to add to the exercise.

Workshop Exercise # 1
(A WOMAN, A WIFE)

DIRECTIONS:

1. Search the selected verses and identify the biblical principles described. In your group break-out session make a list of the principles found (20 minutes)
2. Privately identify the principles you are presently applying in your relationship as a woman and, or a wife. Briefly explain how you are fulfilling each principle. (10 minutes)
3. Identify the principles you are not fulfilling. Describe a brief plan for how you intend to fulfill them. Be prepared to share at your discretion. (10 minutes)

Bible Scripture	Biblical Qualities	Applying	Not Applying
Proverbs 31:10	-rare to find a virtuous wife -is of great value		
Proverbs 31:11	-earned her husband's trust -doesn't need to skim		
Proverbs 31:12	-is loyal to him -honors him		
Proverbs 31:13	-self-sufficient to do her housework		
Proverbs 31:14	-wise about finances		

Proverbs 31:15	-meets needs of the family		
Proverbs 31:16	-wise in business		
Proverbs 31:17	-is not afraid to do hard work		
Proverbs 31:18	-keeps herself looking well -does not pass out at night		
Proverbs 31:20	-is kind and giving		
Proverbs 31:23	-makes her husband proud		
Proverbs 31:25	-is covered in honor		
Proverbs 31:26	-is wise and careful about what she speaks		
Proverbs 31:31	-is revered by others		

WORKSHOP EXERCISE #2
(EMPLOYEE)

DIRECTIONS:

1. Search the selected verses and identify the biblical principles described. In your group break-out session make a list of the principles found (20 minutes)

Bible Scripture	Biblical Qualities	Applying	Not Applying
Exodus 21:5	-faithfulness		
Ephesians 6:5	-obedience		
Colossians 3:22	-loyalty and professionalism		
I Timothy 6:1	-respect		
Titus 2:9	-desire to please		
1 Peter 2:18	-patience in hard times		

2. Privately identify the principles you are presently applying in your relationship as a woman and, or a wife. Briefly explain how you are fulfilling each principle. (10 minutes)
3. Identify the principles you are not fulfilling. Describe a brief plan for how you intend to fulfill them. Be prepared to share at your discretion. (10 minutes)

Workshop Exercise #3
(EMPLOYER)

DIRECTIONS:

1. Search the selected verses and identify the biblical principles described. In your group break-out session make a list of the principles found (20 minutes)
2. Privately identify the principles you are presently applying in your relationship as a woman and, or a wife. Briefly explain how you are fulfilling each principle. (10 minutes)
3. Identify the principles you are not fulfilling. Describe a brief plan for how you intend to fulfill them. Be prepared to share at your discretion. (10 minutes)

Bible Scripture	Biblical Qualities	Applying	Not Applying
Deuteronomy 24:15	-prompt payment of wages		
Job 31:13-14	-consideration for employees		
Ephesians 6:9	-refrain from threats		
Colossians 4:1	-deal justly		

WORKSHOP EXERCISE #4
(CHILD)

DIRECTIONS:

1. Search the selected verses and identify the biblical principles described. In your group break-out session make a list of the principles found (20 minutes)
2. Privately identify the principles you are presently applying in your relationship as a woman and, or a wife. Briefly explain how you are fulfilling each principle. (10 minutes)
3. Identify the principles you are not fulfilling. Describe a brief plan for how you intend to fulfill them. Be prepared to share at your discretion. (10 minutes)

Bible Scripture	Biblical Qualities	Applying	Not Applying
Psalms 34:11	-to fear the Lord		
Proverbs 10:1	-make parents glad		
Proverbs 20:11	-do pure and right works		
Proverbs 23:22	-pay attention to your father and do not despise your mother		
Ecclesiastes 12:1	-remember God		
Mark 7:10	-honor your parents		

Ephesians 6:1	-obey your parents		
Proverbs 1:8	-pay attention to instructions from your mother and father		

WORKSHOP EXERCISE #5
(PARENT)

DIRECTIONS:

1. Search the selected verses and identify the biblical principles described. In your group break-out session make a list of the principles found (20 minutes)
2. Privately identify the principles you are presently applying in your relationship as a woman and, or a wife. Briefly explain how you are fulfilling each principle. (10 minutes)
3. Identify the principles you are not fulfilling. Describe a brief plan for how you intend to fulfill them. Be prepared to share at your discretion. (10 minutes)

Bible Scripture	Biblical Qualities	Applying	Not Applying
Deuteronomy 6:7	-duty to teach		
Proverbs 22:6	-duty to train		
2 Corinthians 12:14	-provide for		
Ephesians 6:4	-nurture		
Timothy 3:4	-control over		
Titus 2:4	-give love		
Proverbs 13:24	-to correct		
Proverbs 19:18	-discipline		

WORKSHOP EXERCISE #6
(FRIEND)

DIRECTIONS:

1. Search the selected verses and identify the biblical principles described. In your group break-out session make a list of the principles found (20 minutes)
2. Privately identify the principles you are presently applying in your relationship as a woman and, or a wife. Briefly explain how you are fulfilling each principle. (10 minutes)
3. Identify the principles you are not fulfilling. Describe a brief plan for how you intend to fulfill them. Be prepared to share at your discretion. (10 minutes)

Bible Scripture	Biblical Qualities	Applying	Not Applying
Galatians 5:22-23 (list each fruit of the spirit and describe how you produce that fruit in your relationship)	-Fruit of the spirit love joy peace long suffering gentleness goodness faith meekness temperance		
Proverbs 17:17 Proverbs 18:24	-loves at all times -loyalty		
Proverbs 27:10	-cherish old friendships		

Proverbs 27:17	-a source for refinement		
Ecclesiastes 4:9	-work together		
I Samuel 18:1	-bound together deeply		
2 Corinthians 2:13	-seek after one another		

Workshop Exercise #7
(A MAN, A HUSBAND)

DIRECTIONS:

1. Search the selected verses and identify the biblical principles described. In your group break-out session make a list of the principles found (20 minutes)
2. Privately identify the principles you are presently applying in your relationship as a woman and, or a wife. Briefly explain how you are fulfilling each principle. (10 minutes)
3. Identify the principles you are not fulfilling. Describe a brief plan for how you intend to fulfill them. Be prepared to share at your discretion. (10 minutes)

Bible Scripture	Biblical Qualities	Applying	Not Applying
Proverbs 22:2	-all are made equal		
Galatians 3:28	-no distinction in humanity		
Job 32:8	-inspiration and understanding from God		
Genesis 2:24	-separation from everything to be with his wife		
Ecclesiastes 9:9	-live joyfully with wife		
Ephesians 5:25	-love your wife		
1 Peter 3:7	-honor your wife		

Deuteronomy 6:7	-to teach the children		
2 Corinthians	-provide for family		
Ephesians 6:4	-nurture the children		
1 Timothy 3:4	-control over children		
Proverbs 13:24	-apply correction		

BIBLIOGRAPHY

BIBLES:

1. The Holy Bible, Authorized King James Version, World Publishing, Iowa Falls, IA, USA. "Scriptures used by permission"

2. New American Standard Bible, Foundation Publications, Inc.,

Copyright 1998 by the Lockman Foundation, Anaheim, CA "Scripture taken from the New American Standard Bible @,

Copyright 1960, 1962, 1963, 1968, 1971, 1972, 1973,1975, 1977, 1995, by The Lockman Foundation. Used by permission. www. Lockman.org

3. New International Version, Bible Soft PC Study Bible@ Version 4, Copyright 1998—2003, Bible Soft, Inc.

REFERENCES:

1. Young'sAnalytical Concordance To The Bible, Robert Young, LL.D., Thomas Nelson Publishers, New York, 1982

2. A Critical Lexicon and Concordance to The English and Greek New Testament, Bullinger, Ethelbert W., First Zondervan Printing, Grand Rapids, MI, 1975

3. The Thompson Chain-Reference Bible, 5th Ed, B. B. Kirkbride Bible Co., Inc., Indianapolis, IN, USA, 1982

4. Holman Bible Dictionary, Butler, Trent C., Gen. Ed., Holman Bible Publishers, Nashville, TN, 1991

5. George Muller: Man of Faith and Miracles (Men of Faith). Miller, Basil. Published by Bethany House Publishers, 1972. ISBN 10: 0871231824

www.ingramcontent.com/pod-product-compliance
Lightning Source LLC
Chambersburg PA
CBHW021629120626
46545CB00002B/464